Representing Yourself in Court:

The Risks and Rewards of Practicing Pro-Se Law

By: Rich Bergeron

CHAPTER ONE:

Accepting the Challenge and Assessing the Risks

The situation is already upon you. A lawsuit is imminent, already in motion, or something you feel you have to file on your own. That's probably why you're reading this.

You've looked at the cost of hiring a lawyer, and you're baffled at how much one can charge before he or she even steps into a courtroom on your behalf. "What can a lawyer do that I can't do," you may ask yourself.

If you truly do have the time and energy to devote to a legal battle, you are your own best witness and the ultimate bearer of truth. Yet, it's not all sunshine and lollipops in the legal world. As your own attorney you may set the strategy, handle the paperwork, and line up the evidence, but you also take all the blame if you fail.

Every now and then a pro-se party launches an incredible effort, though. Consider the case of the 2008 movie "*Flash of Genius*" and the main character Bob Kearns. Here's the original article about his story: http://nyr.kr/1uHxtxs.

If you are sincere enough and have a cause of action and/or a defense that is compelling enough, there could be an article or a movie about you someday. If not, the only movie starring you will be the one in your head… playing over and over again like a broken record. That's the horror story, the one where you go down in flames in the end because you bit off more than you could chew.

Representing yourself is not a choice to take lightly. Judges will look at you cross-eyed. They will be grumpy when you don't have the ability to match your opponent in professional courtesy and background knowledge in basic law. They will tell you to get a lawyer as much as they can. They will chastise you whenever you may stumble in your understanding of the law and your execution of the archaic traditions of the court. You will need to keep your cool and maintain your focus while trying your hardest to imitate a real lawyer.

Researching, properly documenting, and placing the facts and the law that support you on the record in a language and manner the opposing counsel and the judge will understand and certify takes a tremendous amount of time and effort for most cases. This is especially true if you start out with absolutely no knowledge of the legal profession. You may need a loyal assistant who will work for pennies or for free. If you have a big enough case your opposition might have an army of researchers and clerks. The paperwork alone can often be the most frustrating part of the process.

Cases do not typically resolve themselves in a few months. Civil and criminal cases can both take decades to come to an official conclusion. Sometimes cases sit in limbo for years. If no party chooses to proceed with a motion or status hearing, the two parties can keep a case going as long as they want in some rare instances. Sharp lawyers can slow things down or speed things up in the process on a dime, and they can leave you in the dust before you know what's happening. Mounting an offense in the face of an aggressive lawyer who wants to grind you by slowing the court process down or speeding it up suddenly can be tricky. This is where crafty paperwork and unique creativity come in handy.

The risks can be tremendous in criminal proceedings. Without prior legal experience it is an impossible task to go into criminal court thinking you can wrangle your way out of a guilty finding. Unless it is a case with minimal consequences, I would not recommend passing on a public defender or paid counsel in a criminal proceeding. If it is a matter of necessity, you have no choice. Just don't expect any judges to eat out of your hand. You'll have to win them over with your compassion for getting it right, abiding by all the rules, and not making rookie mistakes.

As someone with no official 9 to 5 job and a profound understanding of writing and the English language, getting sued for $25 million was a perfect excuse for me to go through my own informal law school. I had the time, the dedication, and the energy to see it through. My case is unique. So is yours. If you have the facts on your side, getting them on the record properly can be a real challenge when you go in with no prior experience.

This book is primarily geared toward the people caught up out there in the civil legal channels. I'm hoping to reach all the folks like me. I had little time to understand and confront the process. The case against me was flimsy at best. The attorney who drafted the initial complaint based all his claims on fabricated evidence. There was no way I could stand by and allow a charge of defamation to stand against me unchallenged. I reported what I knew and what my sources told me. I had court documents in hand and witness testimony for multiple stories.

I needed this book myself back then. That early stage gave me the feeling of a "me against the world" situation, and I had to learn how to fight back quickly. There were a ton of sleepless nights spent trying to figure out how to mount an effective defensive front.

Even if you strike first in the legal process, you go in as a pro-se party with one foot already deep in quicksand. It requires a surprising amount of time and effort to make any headway at all in this environment.

Yet, somehow, the facts I presented began to win over judges. I beat the technicalities, and I proved my case worthy of one contentious hearing after another. Just when I would warm up to one judge, I would get another one who had no clue what I'd been through prior to meeting him. You don't get a fresh start with an old-school judge.

Judge Lloyd King, an import from Hawaii, seemed to despise me from the start for representing myself in federal bankruptcy court in Las Vegas. I will never forget the first day I realized he would be presiding over my case. It was the first hearing I appeared at in person, thinking it would conclude the case. The judge was furious and demanded I attend every hearing after that. I traveled from Boston to attend this one hearing and ended up staying in Las Vegas nearly two years before the conclusion of the proceedings allowed me to return home. My checkmate move turned into a stalemate. Judge King called me out for having my own advantages, and it made me think I needed to use more of those advantages outside of court to help close the case. Ol' Lloyd even admitted in open court to not reading the bulk of the pleadings in my case at one hearing.

There are Judge Kings everywhere, and they will always favor trained attorneys. These judges often rationalize ignoring your contributions by concluding that they have better things to do than read your attempts at writing legal motions. The system may seem corrupt at every turn, but if you have patience and the will to fight to the end, you can succeed in court as your own attorney. If you run across a Judge King in your own legal adventures, you just may have to give yourself a crash course on the appeals process for your particular jurisdiction.

If you still think you can beat the overwhelming odds against you succeeding as your own attorney, proceed with caution. This is not a test of the Emergency Broadcast System. This is for keeps. You are expected to know the law and all the procedures, even if you do have to teach yourself. It doesn't matter to the judge that your opposing counsel went to Harvard. The process is unfair and based on wealth, and everyone knows it. Your judge used to be a lawyer himself. You'll need to show him something he hasn't seen out of your kind before. You need to bring the "WOW" factor. You must show him exactly why you don't need a lawyer and why you would only be handcuffed by one.

If your particular case is not grounded in sound law, it won't last very long in any court. Research the law. Seek out free consultations with real attorneys first as much as possible. String them along like you're looking to hire them. They might just tell you everything you need to know. The Supreme Court and the US Court of Appeals have already decided just about any issue you can think of that would result in a lawsuit. You just have to find examples that support your cause of action. Precedent cases will make or break your performance as a self-represented party.

If you can spend the time and energy, have a certain level of organization and competency with writing, and are willing to play on an uneven field of battle, then representing yourself might even be fun. Just don't make that leap without some deep thought. Legal boot camp is not fun if you've never had to operate in that environment before. What you think is an intriguing challenge going in could end up being the worst nightmare you've ever experienced.

If you're still willing to soldier on despite the odds, there are actually some advantages to representing yourself. Some of them may surprise you.

CHAPTER TWO:

Embracing the Advantages

You are not a law firm. You have limitations, and the law actually affords you some leeway in getting up to speed on the whole legal process:

The special concern for the pro se litigant is not limited to the pleading stage. **Both at trial and on appeal, he is to be spared "the harsh application of technical rules."** _Traguth v. Zuck_, 710 F.2d at 95; _Bates v. Jean_, 745 F.2d at 1150. (Emphasis added.)

Judges who scorn you for going it alone may forget their charge to respect your position and give you some extra room to make mistakes and figure things out. You can't "play dumb" in pleadings or in court, but what could be a catastrophic mistake for a trained lawyer could and should be forgiven by most fair judges when it comes from you.

For every statute and precedent case that tells judges to be respectful of a pro-se party's uphill battle, there are others saying that self-represented parties are still expected to know the law. Don't overplay your hand in asking for ridiculous allowances for coloring outside the lines. Don't fail to research all the background law and then claim you need extra time to figure it all out. Know the ins and outs of every legal argument before you make it in a pleading or in court.

Most courts will allow you to submit most of your defensive or offensive pleadings on paper, and if the venue is too far away many courts have telephonic-appearance-capable courtrooms. This is a one-front war most lawyers are used to fighting strictly through the court system alone. What your opposition typically has that you don't is money to spend, education on the system, and experience. You have to embrace a second front of battle to have any chance at victory.

There can be an equalizer for self-represented parties, especially when the court seems especially biased. Shine the media spotlight on the corruption you see, or expose the court's failure to give you a fair shake. If you can't get traditional media channels excited about your cause, toot your own horn.

Consider Hank Mishkoff and http://www.taubmansucks.com/. Most law firms and lawyers don't have the time or passion to get word out about their cause unless it's a huge pharmaceutical corporation they're after and they want to know if you used their bad product (i.e. 1-800-BAD-DRUG). The power of social media is exponentially expanding. It is easier than ever to craft your own personal Web-site. There are tons of domain names out there that are available for the taking at very affordable prices. If your story can't generate traditional media headlines, make your own headlines. Just make sure your site paints the best picture of the truth possible. Back it up with evidence. Make sure the right people see it.

Online activism became so important to my cases that I created a resource site for what are now called "gripe sites." http://www.suckssite.com is filled with interesting links and content that can help you understand the legal background and requirements of a "sucks site." First of all, the cardinal rule is you can't be selling anything "confusingly similar" to the product or service of the person you are trying to "parody" or target with your site. This is one of the reasons the sucks site is used. You can't confuse your page with the real thing when you use that word in the domain name.

THE Online Community For Protest Against Injustice

The best course is to sell nothing at all on your gripe site, but you could ask for donations to your legal fund. Just tell the story, and take lessons from Mr. Mishkoff. Keep the story on track, and make it compelling. If it is a solid, blockbuster tale of corruption and greed, it will sell itself. If you have a catchy domain and can get it out there with a viral explosion, your opposition will feel the gut punch from the bad publicity hit.

One of the main advantages to taking your story online is the freedom of publication. Beyond what is even admissible in most court rooms, the press has the power to illuminate everything. My own foray into the legal process came on the heels of me getting sued for $25 million for writing the true history of Xyience, Incorporated (see www.xyiencesucks.com). I fought back, and there came a time when I had some discussions with the company's co-CEOs just before the whole outfit went bankrupt.

I taped the phone call on one occasion (http://pro-seblog.com/wp-content/uploads/2014/12/frankandsanford.mp3). These two business men obviously wanted to patch things up with me. At one point in the call both of them openly admitted that they went to my Web-site to try to find out the real history of the company. The court unfortunately would not allow the tape to be used as evidence (considered part of settlement negotiations), but it's Exhibit A in the court of public opinion. The laws on publication are very different than the laws on admissibility as evidence in court.

Even if I obtained the tape illegally, I could still publish it legally or at least make a novel argument for why publication was in the interest of exposing the truth. Consider the case of *CBS, Inc., et al v. Davis*, 510 U.S. 1315. The court battle pitted the producers of the documentary series "*48 Hours*" against the owners of a meat packing plant. Plant owners claimed that a video tape of their factory's shady operations did not come into the network's hands legally. They sought to shut down the airing of the footage by seeking an emergency stay, but the resulting denial of that request became a monumental case for journalistic activism and investigative reporting. You can read more on this vital precedent case here: http://supreme.justia.com/cases/federal/us/510/1315/ (You can also find a variety of other important cases regarding free speech contained within the document).

Another case involving stolen documents opened up a scandal that led to the censure of a Senator from Connecticut back in 1967. Senator Thomas J. Dodd served "The Constitution State" from 1959 to 1971, dying just months after finishing out his final term as senator. Proven to be using campaign funds for personal expenses, the Senator was also the target of a newspaper column based on documents purportedly stolen from Dodd's office. The documents were copied and smuggled out rather than removed permanently from the office so Dodd could no longer access them himself. The civil charge of conversion did not apply. The publication of the documents was entirely legal according to the chain of appeals on this case. Though they could not be used as direct evidence for a criminal probe or as evidence for use in civil claims, the incriminating secrets of the congressman represented a solid background for further investigation. The public interest was served by exposing Dodd's shortcomings and abuse of public office.

Here is a link to one of the scathing articles on Dodd published by the St. Petersburg Times and written by Jack Anderson and Drew Pearson, the plaintiffs in the landmark case of *Pearson v. Dodd*, 410 F.2d 701(D.C. Cir.), *cert. denied*, 395 U.S. 947 (1969): http://bit.ly/1l8xzqr. Here is another link to some of the important records and details of the case: http://bit.ly/1jkwcFz.

If you really want to get excited about exposing important secrets, research the case of Daniel Ellsberg, who is a former United States military analyst. During Ellsberg's tenure with The Rand Corporation, he released what came to be known as "The Pentagon Papers" in 1971. There are books written about the resulting turmoil and the laws and legal nuances Ellsberg used to avoid serious prosecution. The whole political landscape in America changed as a result of Ellsberg's disclosures. The government's own overzealous and incompetent crusade against Ellsberg collapsed under its own impossible weight when the trial revealed corruption at every turn. Though it takes some liberties with the actual facts of the story, the best way to learn the framework of this saga is to watch the 2003 movie *The Pentagon Papers* starring James Spader as Ellsberg.

Your right of publication is undisputed. Use it to your advantage.

There are also tactics you can use that traditional lawyers wouldn't think of or are incapable of resorting to if they want to keep their licenses to practice. Dirty tricks like hacking into a company's mainframe and reading all their pertinent documents wouldn't be condoned by any reputable legal firm. Yet, it's an entirely different legal realm when someone within the company itself shares the login information and tells you what to look for. Emails can also create real smoking guns in civil cases, so if you can get a hold of an incriminating one you can verify, it could be all downhill for your opposition. Even if you can't use intercepted communications as direct legal evidence, you can often publish those missives as proof of what your enemy is plotting against you.

For instance, I once obtained a direct recording of an official company meeting where I was a topic of discussion. This was due to me directly contact Xyience employees by email. Since the company's president at the time was a gentleman named John Lennon, I called the blog entry that included the recording: The Lost Lennon Tapes. All kidding aside, Mr. Lennon's comments about me almost amounted to defamation. Publishing his rant about me was even better than suing him, though. The fact that the head honcho of the company was bringing me up in a meeting and seemed genuinely worried about people working with me was huge for my case.

You also have rights to traditional discovery requests as a pro-se party, so you can seek much of your evidence through proper channels. This should not stop you from acting as your own private investigator or hiring out this work if you can afford it. I recruited a company insider to mine my information for me. I could watch Xyience's active surveillance video, read their emails, and see all their sales projections. I gained more material this way and through direct communication with employees than I could possibly learn by asking the judge to approve my requests. I also had the ability to review financial records turned in by the legal teams my opposition hired to escape liability for their actions. Hundreds of thousands of dollars were devoted to defending against my case.

I also learned that there were efforts costing tens of thousands of dollars to move Xyience's company Web-sites ahead of my gripe site, and once it became apparent that I was able to infiltrate their computer system the company spent more thousands trying to figure out a way to keep me out. For the better part of the battle, my site ranked third in a Google search for Xyience, and I didn't have to pay anybody to maintain that slot.

I went after the most culpable parties in the Xyience scandal with more aggression than I've ever displayed in any other case. I had no way to get home at the end of the legal battle and no excuse to avoid my responsibility to get to the bottom of the story. I contacted many of these parties at their homes and through their official emails. I sent word up through the company itself about my military training. One security guard at Xyience headquarters actually received orders to watch YouTube videos of my boxing workouts because they wanted him to be prepared in case I showed up to fight. It felt good to know they were the ones with all the money and the lawyers, but I was the one who was causing them to panic and worry about what I might do next.

People used to ask me if I was afraid I was going to "get whacked" for pursuing the casino barons behind the Xyience bankruptcy. After all, I exposed their family history, which included some direct links to organized crime. By the time I left Las Vegas, the opposing big shot lawyer for the billionaire casino owners was literally begging the judge to allow *him to help me* pay for my plane ticket home. He had no problems admitting he wanted no part of the fight I was waging against him and his clients. Sometimes you really have to flip the script.

Even if I never won in principle in my fierce crusade to bring Lorenzo and Frank Fertitta III to task for victimizing hundreds of innocent Xyience investors, the creative war is still ongoing. You see, the court battle is only part of the whole picture. Even if you lose it, you still have the backdrop for the bigger story: your effort to expose the truth publicly. It's hard to "sex up" (http://www.fightopinion.com/2009/12/30/scandals-in-mma-and-dont-forget-about-xyience/) a story like Xyience and make it palatable for the general public to really get excited about it. Still, anyone can get behind an underdog who gives it his best shot in a case like mine and secures at least some small moral victory in the process.

My personal research in another case connected Federal Judge Sarah Evans Barker to a major conglomerate called Clarian Health Care. The judge seemed overly biased in her rulings for Dr. Barry Eppley in a case he filed with an intent to silence my book about a woman who alleged that the plastic surgeon committed serious negligence. At the time the case entered the federal court system, I did not have a word of this book written yet. All I had was a set of voluminous notes from my interviews with the vociferous and determined victim.

The plastic surgeon dragged me into the case by basically trying to inhibit any "future speech" on the subject of this questionable operation he performed on a woman named Lucille Iacovelli. I was not a named party, but he managed to include my name in an injunction forbidding me from writing about the operation. Iacovelli was also the subject of a documentary on HBO called *Plastic Disasters*. I actually saw the documentary before meeting Lucille, and it intrigued me. Just months after seeing that documentary film, I responded to an ad Lucille placed on Craigslist asking for a writer's help on a book she wanted to write.

A bit of online research and a few phone calls led me to paperwork proving that the doctor paid his practice insurance to a Clarian Health Care company, paid his facility rent to a Clarian company, and practiced nearly his entire career under the Clarian management umbrella.

Judge Sarah Evans Barker has a family history dating back nearly a century in health care in the Indianapolis area. She was also on the board of directors for Clarian Health Care at the time of the Eppley case. I demanded she recuse herself, but she denied all my requests. I worked with Dr. Eppley's former patient to defend her First Amendment rights, but the corruption was overwhelming.

I even registered www.judgegod.com to expose Judge Barker and her kangaroo court mentality. She didn't take long to shut it down, disregarding the constitution she is supposed to defend even when it offends her own sense of pride. I also registered www.legaldunce.com, www.eppleyplasticsurgerysucks.com and www.scarletlawyer.com, all of which are now defunct. If you still want to see what these sites looked like, there are some crude copies of the old framework available when you look each domain up at: https://web.archive.org. I will touch more on this resource later in the book. The following images are examples of some of the content placed on those sites to get my point across in an entertaining fashion.

The opposing forces you will face in your legal battles will always have their own advantages over you. Still, the pen and the artist brush can be much more powerful than the sword or the pocketbook. Lawyers and judges don't typically resort to publicizing their own efforts, but you can and should use this front to help put pressure on your opposition that you simply cannot put on them through traditional legal channels. There's no excuse to fail to use this advantage you have as a self-represented party.

You may not realize you have another leg up on your duly represented competition. If you don't have a ton of cash at your disposal, you are both judgment-proof and more likely use your funds wisely. Corrupt individuals and corporations know that having excellent lawyers is the difference between criminal court and civil court. They will throw money at lawyers all day long if that's what it takes to avoid culpability or even a hint of a scandal. Chances are, if you are facing serious difficulties, you have an opponent who is well funded and serious about winning at all costs. This is sometimes a benefit, because many lawyers who have such padded expense accounts will spend too much money on useless endeavors.

Even better for you, they might be going through the motions and simply trying to accumulate some serious billable hours without any real regard for where the case is going. Lawyers like this will underestimate you at the same time, swatting you around like a barn cat toying with a dying field mouse. If you work hard enough at your own craft, you can really surprise a firm that overplays their hand or gets too wrapped up in filling the docket with paperwork designed to overwhelm you.

This is where you often have to use Goliath's own strength against himself. Act like you borrowed the American Express card your opponent puts all his or her business expenses on. Make those lawyers work. Call them up and have conversations with them. Send detailed emails they have to review and respond to. Run up that padded bill for your ruthless foe. File copious documents if you can, but make sure they are all well-founded in law. Every hour of work these lawyers do comes out of the pocket of your opposition in most cases. Many of these lawyers charge a minimum of $100 per hour. Turn hundreds of hours into thousands of hours, and the clients of these schmucks will start to blow a gasket.

If the lawyers are helping their clients cover up corrupt activity, blow up their spots, too. I had no problem calling out my capable but corruptible legal opposition over the years.

I once sincerely told a judge that Las Vegas Attorney Greg Garman liked to twist the facts for the court like a clown twisting balloon animals for kids at a birthday party. I almost went as far as getting a huge clown cutout with Garman's name on it to hang outside the courtroom the day of a hearing.

Indiana Attorney Todd Richardson crusaded for the wrong cause in my case, but his Harvard degree didn't stop me from making him the main model for my legaldunce.com logo above. If I had a judge with a clear conscience and no health care bias, I might have had a shot at beating Richardson.

Then there was Peter J. Aspesi (the guy with the L on his forehead in the above graphic). Aspesi is one of the most incompetent legal representatives I ever had the misfortune of meeting in person. He also has the distinction of being the only person I ever came close to punching in a public courtroom. That scene unfolded when he helped a psychotic woman (see http://www.arlenemulleysucks.com/) sue Lucille Iacovelli less than a week after her suicide. The story of Aspesi and his maniacal client could fill the pages of a whole series of books. Suffice it to say there should be a picture of this guy next to the word "shady" in the dictionary.

A guy like Aspesi is fairly easy to rattle, and a client like his will soon run out of money. Just like the first lawyer from Xyience who filed suit against me, Aspesi crapped out fairly quickly. The legal bills of both suckers went unpaid. As a pro-se party your bills are minimal, but your time is still valuable. What can seem like a deficit you can't overcome in the beginning will actually sometimes work as a benefit in the end. If you make under a certain amount, you can also have the majority of your filing fees paid for by the court. You also don't have to cloud your focus on the case because you have to work on someone else's case. Your attention and passion is wrapped up in this one case, and you can devote as much time to it as it takes to win.

Another advantage that may not seem so special at first is that you don't have to win against the right competition. Sometimes winning is just an extra benefit of pushing back and standing up for yourself. The fight against the system, the rage against the machine, and the bucking of the establishment is the real story you're trying to get across. You don't need to destroy anyone to gain a spiritual victory. Just pushing their buttons for a while and fighting the good fight is noble if it agitates your opposition enough.

Just hanging in there as long as I did against prominent law firms in two different states seemed impressive enough to me for me to be proud of myself. Along the way there were articles written about my struggles and my causes, and Fox News LA even did a television interview with me on the plastic surgery case:

http://www.myfoxla.com/story/18419056/the-truth-behind-plastic-surgery

Even though judges only ruled in my favor a handful of times, I made all those little victories count. You can do the same. Just be creative and respect the law. Don't publish anything you can't defend in court.

CHAPTER THREE:

Researching the Rules, Customs, and Precedent Cases

Effective legal work never goes down in real life the way you see it portrayed on television or in movie theaters. That's not to say you can't learn something about how Hollywood makes the law seem more appealing and artistic than it actually is. Some important legal dramas—both real and fictional—have defined generations. Think of the iconic Jack Nicholson line that begins with, "You can't handle the truth!" You know what movie I'm talking about already, before I even name it.

A Few Good Men is a modern classic with multiple imbedded legal lessons about patience, standing up to authority, setting up questions for witnesses, and overcoming amazing obstacles to get at the truth. It's not about you or me, though. It's not an applicable situation to anything the "Average Joe" is dealing with in court today. Still, we can use the same tactics and techniques that worked for Tom Cruise's character in our own individual cases.

If you have the time, watching legal television shows and movies can actually give you ideas and get you somewhat familiar with how the legal process generally works. Just keep in mind most of what you are seeing is glamorized and dramatized. I definitely recommend the 2008 movie "*Flash of Genius*" that I mentioned in Chapter One. It is the Holy Grail of self-represented legal performances, and it is all based on a true story.

For a more popular drama about criminal law and self-representation, check out the film "*Fracture*" with Anthony Hopkins and Ryan Gosling. Although the character Hopkins plays is no role model by any means, he uses his "disadvantages" as a self-represented party to run circles around a young assistant district attorney played by Ryan Gosling.

If you need more of a "feel-good" cause to get excited about, the best two movies are "*Conviction*" from 2010 and "*A Civil Action*" from 1998. These are your best two examples of fighting the good fight to the bitter end.

"*Conviction*" stars Hillary Swank as the sister of a man (played by Sam Rockwell) wrongfully convicted of murder. She puts herself through law school to help prove his innocence. It is a heartfelt story of one of life's best lessons: *The truth always shines through in the end*. It is also a profile in perseverance, highlighting the need for a certain level of dedication to exhausting every channel of possible relief.

"*A Civil Action*" is a "based on a true story" drama. The action surrounds a monumental pollution case with John Travolta starring as a slick personal injury lawyer who gets in way over his head against hotshot corporate interests. Travolta's opposition in the film is trying to hide serious leaks and spills of volatile chemicals. The factories and industries producing the chemicals caused a perfect storm of town water contamination, resulting in multiple cancers sweeping through affected neighborhoods. Travolta's opposition includes an old and wise litigator played masterfully by Robert Duval. It is worth the watch, and one of the most potent lessons it teaches is not to overplay your hand.

You can also watch a number of television legal dramas and comedies like "*Suits*," "*Law & Order*" and "*Boston Legal.*" I'm sure there are also other movies and shows that are just as inspiring, funny and/or exciting. Just don't follow any lead that is too outrageous or totally uncalled for in your own personal legal situation.

For the serious research, go straight to the "Rules of Local Procedure" for whatever district, circuit, or county court system you are called before. These lists of requirements, customs and courtesies can be chock full of crucial information. Fail to read and understand them, and even a lenient judge might scold you in open court.

Once you figure out what the rules are on what motions you can file and when, you will want to think about all that paperwork necessary to make a solid case. If you've been sued, you typically file an answer, and maybe if you are really aggressive a motion to dismiss and/or a counterclaim will go out at the same time. All this must typically be paired with real, relevant evidence and affidavits to certify that evidence as genuine. If you are suing another party or group of parties, you'll need a complaint, evidence and supporting witness affidavits. Often civil cases are won on the paperwork alone. Opposing lawyers also sometimes literally attempt to bury the other side in an avalanche of paperwork, and the best attorneys can make it all appear related to the case at hand.

Criminal cases are likely the most popular realm for a self-represented party practice in. An inmate, or someone who is soon to be one, has little resources to spend on a law firm or even one half-way decent public defender. There are specific rules of criminal procedure for different jurisdictions as well. Study these closely, and keep them in mind when you formulate your strategy and put together your paperwork.

If you are incarcerated, get your hands on whatever resources you can, and reach out to any fellow inmate who might be known for some degree of success with his jailhouse lawyering. Above all, know your rights and inform the judge at hearings when your rights are infringed upon by your jailers and/or prosecutors.

Family Court likely comes in second on the list of courts where parties represent themselves most often. Custody battles, divorce and separation matters and other family disputes are in their own special category somewhere between civil and criminal law.

Small Claims Court also features a majority of self-represented parties. This realm of low-stakes legal wrangling has long been the fodder for TV Judges like Joe Brown, Joseph Wapner, and Judy Sheindlin.

All of these areas of law have their own set of rules, customs, and procedures. There are all kinds of offshoots, too. There's patent law, trademark law, First Amendment law, contract law, business law, etcetera.

Of course, we certainly can't forget the mother of all legal playing fields: Appeals Court. That's the place your case ends up when you're not happy with the outcome and see an angle to reverse it. Depending on how high up the chain of judging command you go with appeals, this stage is typically much more strict and rigid with paperwork and customs than any other area of law. A sound legal case needs to be built so that it can handle the challenge of a sincere appeal attempt by a skilled attorney.

The best way to find out the history and general structure of your kind of case is to look up your issue and realm of law and search for a similar case online. It helps to find a successful case. It doesn't have to be from the same general neighborhood where you reside, but sometimes that helps as well. If you have a few dollars to spend on research, the absolute best place to turn is http://www.pacer.gov/ (Public Access to Court Electronic Records). You can apply for a password to this system with a credit card, and millions of cases will be at your fingertips.

PACER can be utilized on multiple fronts of action against any well-heeled opponent. If you are focusing on an opponent who has a history of corruption, search his or her name in the legal database. Find out if your opposition is a registered agent for any businesses or if he owns a business with serious litigation history. Often you can find hidden criminal or civil cases you could never find anywhere else online. Sometimes you can even find facts to use against an opposing attorney. If you can find a case where your opposition served on the opposite side of the issue, the precedents they cite in those cases can be critical. You can find the documents for entire cases on PACER. It is an absolute gem, but keep track of your purchases. It is expensive to review thousands of pages on this system. Seek out only what you absolutely need, and try to download only the most crucial documents.

If you are pressing a suit or looking to file a counterclaim, you should also research "Torts" and "Causes of Action." Don't just use Google, either. Try search engines like dogpile.com and document hosting sites like Slideshare and docstoc.com. Find out the federal circuit that handles appeals in your court system. The cases at that level and at Supreme Court level will be your trump cards. The more documents from actual cases you consume, the more you will start thinking like a lawyer who passed the bar on the first try.

Don't forget YouTube University, of course. There are actually numerous self-help videos available on video hosting sites across the Internet. All this knowledge is free, as long as you can afford to use the Internet. You can learn all about presenting your legal argument in the proper legal framework, cross examining witnesses, what to do at a deposition, and any number of other lessons about legal practice. Just search a particular topic you need to brush up on, and you'll likely find tons of material to digest. Always take notice of which videos you liked the best and which ones had the most views when you are perusing these sites. Knowing how and why videos go viral could be crucial to that second front of the war that I will discuss more at the end of the book.

I highly recommend the YouTube profile (https://www.youtube.com/user/lawmed1) of Gerry Oginski if you have a personal injury or medical malpractice case. Even if it's general law tips you are looking for, you can find some great knowledge that comes from a long history of litigation Gerry's been a part of over the years.

One genuine product I also stand by is JURISDICTIONARY. I have a site at http://www.pro-seblog.com with multiple blogs about this amazing technical training program. It includes everything you really need to understand how each crucial stage of the process should unfold if you want your case to be successful. If you choose to take the leap and buy their course, please use my affiliate link:

http://www.jurisdictionary.com/?refercode=BR0004

Jurisdictionary can turn you into a wolf in sheep's clothing when you go into court far better prepared for battle than the opposition or judge expects you to be.

Above all, there is no substitute for experience. Learn from doing as much as possible. Research public speaking and practice your inflection. Rehearse the remarks you plan to use in court in front of an audience before each hearing. Try to limit your commentary to language the judge and opposing counsel will understand. Listen to other court hearings if possible.

Some of your research may be inadmissible in court. This is just a fact of life, and sometimes it seems like an unfortunate flaw in the system. The best part about my own multi-front strategy to litigation is that I could populate my sites with content that I could not use in court to prove my points. Evidence judges in court rooms just cannot consider can still be seen by the general public in most legal scenarios. Win "the hearts and minds" of enough people who might be willing to support and champion your position, and you might even inspire the other side to settle to avoid more backlash:

http://www.buzzfeed.com/jakerossen/insult-and-injury-inside-the-webs-one-sided-war-on-doctors#.hiPMo8mQ9

You may also want to spend some time learning about viral videos and search engine optimization if you want to get the message out about your story. The advent of smart phones and constantly improving tablets and laptops means there are computers everywhere. More and more people are getting their news online and checking out blogs. Reality is stranger than fiction. Find out the best way to get your story across, and get it out to the masses.

Never forget to also do some digging on the judge overseeing your case. Many locales allow lawyers and clients to provide donations to a judge for his or her election campaign without requiring recusal. Some states are worse than others. Nevada can be particularly hairy in this regard (http://articles.latimes.com/2006/jun/14/nation/na-judges14). Anywhere judges are elected, this can be a pitfall of practicing as your own attorney there. If you find out your judge has any other serious question of bias or conflict of interest, getting that judge recused can be the difference in getting a fair hearing or being hung out to dry.

There is monstrous, festering corruption and cronyism in the United States Judicial System. It's enough to make you want to puke if you have a case in the courts that needs to be addressed with the utmost courtesy and consideration for the law and the facts that apply. A judge just may not like you, might have personal issues at stake inspiring a clear bias against you, or just happens to have enough experience with the opposing lawyer and client to believe them over you. There are ways to overcome severe bias if you really know what you're doing and you are willing to spend enough time on an effective appeal.

Still, sometimes a judge's complete disrespect for your point of view can come across in an extremely vicious manner. Judges have feelings, too. They are human, and they will strike back when attacked like most people who do not shy away from a fight when you punch them in the face. They are used to getting their own way and doing what they want to do. They do not like to be challenged, and when someone pushes the wrong buttons of a judge consumed by her own power, this is what happens:

http://docs.justia.com/cases/federal/district-courts/indiana/insdce/1:2009cv00386/22793/150

This why I honestly believe you should never expect to win in court. This is also why the publication avenue often provides a bigger helping of justice in the long run. This is not to say you shouldn't still try to get your best effort on the record. Some of my most eloquent and well-researched pleadings came out of losing appeals efforts. There was no reason for the 7th Circuit judges to deny those appeals other than their overwhelming sympathy for Judge Sarah Evans Barker, who I was trying to recuse from the case for a clear and obvious bias toward the plaintiff. Forcing her to step down would be an indictment on her own sense of judicial responsibility, as it would prove she should have stepped down herself.

Later, I even put together a case for violation of civil rights against Judge Barker, but a few technicalities and jurisdictional issues prevented it from going forward. You can't sue judges and win in the majority of cases, and you can generate a ton of backlash by going after them in the court of public opinion. Though at the time I saw no other choice besides lambasting the judge for being corrupt, in hindsight I know I should have spent more time on the doctor and his attorneys.

My strategy was to get her mad enough to make mistakes and drop rulings on Lucille and I that could not be defended at the appeals level. I knew from experience and research that the only time you can mount an acceptable resistance to a court order is when that order is patently unconstitutional. Every honest effort was failing to sway Judge Barker's obvious and blatant bias. I didn't know what else to do other than offend her to the point of getting her to act out of frustration and revenge, and I knew if she was in that mood she would use junk law and biased assumptions to argue her points.

I eventually came to believe that my only hope to save Lucille's legacy was the appeals court having both a collective conscience and the willingness to protect the First Amendment. The 7th Circuit Court of Appeals displayed neither in their ruling on one of my most important appeals, refusing to even discuss the bulk of the issues and evidence I raised to prove Judge Barker could not objectively weigh the facts of the case under the circumstances.

These "hear no evil, see no evil, speak no evil" justices didn't even come to the concrete understanding that the case was still underway, writing on the record that Judge Barker was already "done" with the case. The case was far from over at the time. In fact, Dr. Eppley still proceeded to sue Lucille long after she was dust in the wind. The suit against Lucille proceeded under Judge Barker's biased guidance far beyond the date of Lucille's suicide, and Judge Barker even let the case be passed over to a guardian for her estate that Lucille would never support if she were alive to object.

The level of cruelty and heartlessness that led to Lucille's demise was the kind of juggernaut that could not stop with her taking herself out on her own terms. Dr. Eppley and his rabid attorneys also tried to erase every trace of evidence that she ever existed. They even sent her documents before her death telling her to preserve all her computers and digital devices, which they claimed they would seize. The only way they could actually do that was through serious and egregious abuse of the civil legal channels. These tactics were never designed to apply to any situation beyond one that jeopardizes national security or would lead to a person's serious injury or death if the items weren't immediately seized. Lucille wasn't going to physically hurt or kill anyone with her computers and cameras. If anything she most likely saved the lives of a few folks who decided against a particularly risky plastic surgery procedure after reading her detailed account of her tragic experience.

The 7th Circuit Court's protection of Judge Barker simply made it easier for anyone who can afford a decent lawyer to violate your civil rights while you're alive and make the world forget you ever had any rights after you're gone.

http://www.theindianalawyer.com/article/print?articleId=25903

Looking back on both the Xyience and Eppley/Iacovelli cases, I realize now that their ultimate value lies in their translation to manuscripts. As much as I fought the good fight against the well-heeled opposition in both scenarios and never lost a fortune in the process, the books that result will always be more relevant to society than the actual body of the cases and the contents of the case dockets. The important thing to remember, though, is sometimes you have to claw through the court battle before you can be comfortable publishing the expose. If you can show right away you can defend yourself and beat the odds, the chances of your opposition suing just to shut you up in the future suddenly become very, very slim.

CHAPTER FOUR:

Formulating the Paperwork

One of the most annoying aspects of representing yourself is trying to figure out how to duplicate the paperwork a trained lawyer typically puts together with ease. There are motions, affidavits, declarations, opposition filings, memorandums of law, etcetera. It's tough to know when to file what sometimes, and traditional word processing software doesn't include legal formatting.

Sometimes you just have to take a page out of the old con man's book. Just cut and paste the proper margins you need (many jurisdictions require a numbered line in your margins) if you can't figure out how to get your favorite word processor to put them in the right place. Sometimes just copying the title page format can be the most difficult aspect. Refer to your rules of procedure if you have to on this front. You can typically use the opposing lawyer's version with some minor adjustments. If you're suing someone on your own in the case, though, you'll have to find other examples to follow from PACER or a detailed internet search.

The most important lesson to keep in mind when writing court documents is that it is not time to novelize the situation. This is not a tale of fiction where embellishment entertains the reader. Getting your case into a court of law means it's factually sound and based on a valid legal argument. It shouldn't require any speculation or glossing over key points. Make your paperwork as concise as possible. Make your points clear to any reader, and be sure that the bare facts support your position.

Many pro-se lawyers fail because of a simple problem people face when they are thrown into unfamiliar situations. If you've ever been the only English speaking person in a crowd of foreigners you needed help from, you know the feeling of standing in a court of law and trying to get a judge to listen to you. You can speak the language you know all you want, but sometimes you have to observe and absorb their customs and courtesies before you attempt to communicate at all.

The tendency is to blurt everything out, tell the long drawn out story that you feel is at the heart of the case. Often this is what judges hate about pro-se parties. People who do this tend to wander off the timeline, giving scatter-brained details that only serve to complicate the whole case.

Keep your facts simple and well-defined. Support your facts with evidence. Include exhibits and reference them in your paperwork. Lawyers tend to be very direct in their pleadings. There's no time for dramatization in most of their writing. Don't get me wrong, creativity can certainly be useful to set yourself apart from the monotony of the complex documents submitted by your opposing counsel. Still, whatever writing tools you use to illustrate your point have to be matched by facts you can prove and the documented, verified evidence that supports them.

Affidavits typically need to be numbered, signed and notarized properly, and they should be given about the same weight as testimony in open court. Each number should state a fact, not an assumption. This is the main building block of your case. Just as you can't build most structures without a strong foundation, you can't have a successful legal case without rock solid affidavits. Your exhibits should be verified by these affidavits. All you have to do is refer to each item and explain the circumstances that make each exhibit applicable to the case.

Motions for relief or consideration should be set up to specifically target what you are seeking from the judge. Typically a motion starts with a brief introduction. You should then state the facts, with references to the exhibits and affidavit lines that prove these facts. Prior proceedings, paperwork and pleadings are often referenced. Judges can't be expected to pick up right where they left off in many cases since they have so much on their plates. It helps to have a statement of where the case is at in the whole process. Go over the docket report and pick out key points where developments in the case happened. Remind the judge what the case started as and what stage it is currently at as you write your motion.

Your statement of facts should be followed by a brief introduction to what you are asking for in your motion. The legal background relating to your request and why it is justified should follow that. Again, following the format of the opposing counsel can be helpful in putting all this paperwork together.

Finally, conclude your motion with a reminder of what you want and a general explanation of why you need it. End with a formal "prayer for relief" or request for consideration. Include a signature line and any applicable exhibits, which you will need to file supporting affidavits and/or declarations for.

Appeals courts require the most painstaking attention to detail when it comes to documentation. Typically you need to make a variety of copies of everything you intend to file, and it all has to be neat and up to each court's particular standards. Everything from page numbers to font size is regulated, and just because you are supposed to get some leeway doesn't mean a judge has to like it. Make one wrong move, and a judge may hold it against you, even if it relates to simple flaws in the documentation you file.

Studying files on PACER from related courts is very useful as you learn the legal process. The paperwork may not make sense at first, but as you move through the process you will pick up nuances of preparing paperwork that lawyers use to keep cases focused on the facts that support their side of the litigation. Not everything will make sense right away. You might have to look up a few words to see what they mean.

It helps to be familiar with legal terms, the rules of evidence, and motion practice. The last thing you want to do is spend days on a motion and supporting documents only to find out the motion itself can't be filed due to a deadline or a technicality. Talk to the court's clerks as much as possible when you have technical questions, but never ask them legal advice.

Another reason you should be concise in your arguments relates to page limits. Many motions have a maximum page limit. You may exceed page limits only with permission from the court, which is rarely granted after a lengthy pleading is filed.

Deposition and discovery paperwork is also crucially important to your case. Typically you are allowed to file "Interrogatories" to get your opposition to answer key questions of fact. The answers you get here could define your whole case. Think of all the legal dramas you've ever seen play out in real life or on television. Often the entire case hinges on catching the losing party in a lie. Posing the right questions in the deposition paperwork gets a version of their facts on paper that you can later use to challenge inconsistencies that surface during cross examinations at future hearings or the trial. If the witness strays from the earlier version, you can remind the person they are under oath and ask if they remembered what they said previously in the deposition. Many people squirm on the stand when you catch them trying to explain a discrepancy like this.

NEVER try to contact the judge directly. There is never any acceptable situation where you write a letter directly to a judge overseeing your case. You can communicate by email and snail mail with opposing counsel, but handle all business you need to address with a judge through his or her designated clerk. Keep all your communication professional. I will discuss the only semi-exception to this rule later in the book.

Proofread all your paperwork repeatedly. Some mistakes might be permissible, but the more polished your writing is, the more likely the judge is to see that you are taking the case seriously. Eliminate all irrelevant rambling. Take out any overly complicated statements and simplify them. Cite facts and evidence wherever and whenever possible. Don't forget to back it all up with legal precedents.

Sometimes a case is so unique that there is no pattern of precedent law to define what should be done in your situation. This is a scenario where "new law" can be made. Be sure to find out if your case may qualify as an opportunity to blaze a new legal frontier, because judges may pay much closer attention to your arguments in these cases. Just like regular folks, judges are also susceptible to boredom and being tired of the same old routine. Take them on a journey where you invite them to make history in a realm of law where change is needed, and you will engage them in a process that immediately becomes more important than most of their other cases.

Remember that every document you sign should be based on the truth as it is known to you, a solid legal argument based in precedent or bent on creating new law, and a sincere and clear path to the relief you request. If you use the legal system for "an improper purpose" such as a means to harassing a rival, you can be held liable for "sanctions."

To avoid the charge of filing "frivolous" paperwork, you need to make sure everything you put in writing is verifiable. If you are the only witness, you need to have your testimony on the record. If you can get an expert to agree with your argument, do it. Use an expert when you are not qualified in a certain area that is crucial to the case. Get your expert to explain his or her position in writing, and get it notarized. If there are other witnesses who can help you, get their affidavits as well.

As far as formatting any content you create for use outside of court, always make sure your creative juices don't cause you to incur more legal headaches. Targeting your opposition in the public eye can be viewed by the courts as bullying in many situations. Personal attacks are less protected than parody, humor, and satire. Misrepresentations of the facts can be framed as defamation and/or slander.

Be careful about how you write any reports about how the case is going. Even if it's unconstitutional, some judges will strike down whole Web-sites and/or impose gag orders. If you can avoid targeting the judge and be sensible about how you portray your opponent, a gripe site can be a great way to call attention to an important case. If the site is removed for improper legal reasons, you can bring further action for the court's violation of your Constitutional rights. Just remember, the least amount of time you have to spend in court the better. I only used the approach I did because the judge on the case was just too far gone. At times it really did seem to me like the lawyer, the doctor and the judge had a meeting before the filing of the case and arranged how it was all going to go down. I imagined a get together like the one with all the bank robbers in *Reservoir Dogs*, except the crew that robbed Lucille's rights to tell her story didn't make any stupid mistakes or run into any bad luck. The moral of the analogy is: do not piss the judge off unless you really have nothing else to lose in the matter at the stage you choose to express your frustration with his or her decisions and final orders.

Above all, remember your audience, and save the dramatics and embellishments for the creative effort to sway the public to care about your case. Use the supporting facts, precedent cases, and tight legal language in your court paperwork to keep the judge convinced you are not a "fool." Standing on firm legal ground means getting the right paperwork on the record, all filled with the most relevant information and evidence to prove your case attached.

If you don't already have one, find a printer/scanner/copier combo for your computer. Make sure you get one with some decent ink prices. For bulk copies, go to a copy shop and pay a few bucks to use someone else's ink. Just use your home unit, use a friend's computer or go to a public library to make the originals. Most high tech copy centers have zip drive readers attached to their copiers, so you don't even have to bring physical copies. Also, do not forget to sign every document that requires a signature. Rather than copy your signature on the original, sign every copy's signature page with a pen containing black ink.

CHAPTER FIVE:

Preparing For Your Appearances

Going before the judge in even the smallest court can be a very frightening prospect for the beginner pro-se party. If you have no public speaking experience, nerves can take over. Your voice will shake, and your knees will quake. This is drama most judges are not used to. Keep your focus on the main objective of the hearing. Don't let the scene and the circumstances overwhelm you.

The judge is not expecting you to whip out remarks like the closing arguments of Jake Brigance, a character in the popular 1996 movie *"A Time to Kill."* You don't have to channel your inner Shakespeare, either. Going in as your own attorney, the judge may even try to lecture you before you begin any remarks. There is not much expected from you, simply because the judge typically will not agree with your decision to represent yourself. To win your case, you have to perform like you actually went to law school.

Use the term "Your Honor" when you address the judge. Call the opposing attorney by his or her proper title and last name. Do not talk over the judge. If you don't know what you are doing, the judge is going to try to steer things in the right direction. A fair judge will recognize you running astray and keep you from making stupid mistakes.

One of my first hearings in court when Xyience sued me for $25 million involved a request for a default judgment. That would have ended the case before it really began. It was my first opportunity to tell the judge I had a dog in the fight. It seemed like a total disaster to me as I slogged through the first proceeding. Even with notes in front of me and speaking by phone, it was intimidating.

Finally the judge ruled in my favor and threw out the request for immediate judgment on behalf of the plaintiff. Still, I paid for my ignorance of court proceedings when I pushed the judge to go further than he needed to. I ended that first hearing apologizing after the judge yelled at me. I was pushing a dead issue, and he'd already ruled in my favor. It was like I was trying to get him to do too much, and I should have been more in tune with what was going on. I continued on in the case, made more appearances and filed extensive counterclaims, but I never forgot that first hearing.

Later in the process, there would be different judges to convince. It always seemed like I would get somewhere with one judge only to see another one put in his place at the next hearing. Don't expect things to go smoothly. It's a real nightmare sometimes. Be prepared to start over with someone else on the bench.

The decorum and proper language of court is important, but there is nothing more sacred than substance in an effective legal presentation. You have to have an argument to make and a leg to stand on. Research the applicable local, national, and even international law if it matters to the case. Back up all your arguments with facts, and point the judge and/or jury to your exhibits every chance you get.

Write out your planned remarks and rehearse them religiously before your hearing. Chances are, some of what you want to say could and should be cut short. Keep the commentary front-loaded with facts and references to key precedent and appeals court cases. Remember what the opposing lawyer can object for. There is actually a Wikipedia page for this:

http://en.wikipedia.org/wiki/List_of_objections_(law)

Also remember that attorneys cannot testify on their own behalf. If you want evidence on the record, you actually have to take the stand in most cases. The same goes for the other side, so you can object if your opposition starts to tell the story for the client without "facts being in evidence."

Don't go too far. One of the best parts of "*A Civil Action*" is when Robert Duval's character tells his law class to object when they wake up if they fall asleep at the defense table. Maybe a trained lawyer can pull that off, but *you* still need a valid reason to object. Use objections when you can to break up an opposing attorney's rhythm, but also use them to poke holes in the case. The first thing an attorney is going to do with a lemon case is try to win it on technicalities. Take away his or her best weapons and expose the truth that favors you, and you will start out with the unexpected advantage.

If you have to question a key witness, most of the time you will need a strategy. Start with softball questions and work your way up to the important stuff. If it's your own witness there may be less to worry about, but you still need to be precise and focused. The other side can object if the testimony is not relevant or goes off on a tangent. Those classic movie scenes where the attorney asks the judge to treat the witness as hostile are not likely to unfold in your case. If a witness is hostile to you, sometimes you don't even need permission to return the favor. Just remember the legal scope of your questioning and what purpose peppering an angry witness can serve. It could just as easily come across as you picking on the witness if everything goes south on you.

If your goal is to show the witness is lying, keep all the person's prior sworn remarks in context during questioning. Most liars will never write down the accepted version of the story that exonerates them or someone they are lying for. It's more likely they will remember the truth or some shady version of the truth. To catch a person in a lie, ask them plenty of questions you already have them on the record answering at other proceedings, and listen for huge discrepancies. Call them on every mistake you can, and see how they react. Some people will indeed explode in a rant like Jack Nicholson's character in "*A Few Good Men.*"

It's all about the way you set up the questioning. Like a person performing a polygraph test needs a baseline, you want the witness answering easy questions early on. You want a low stress level, almost boring the person you want to trap later. That way, when the really important question comes, they won't expect it. This works for friends and foes on the witness stand, because the idea is to end with the dramatic effect that will stay with the jury or judge. If you need to pull heart strings or inspire animosity toward a subject, proper questioning on the stand can be crucial.

It may seem like a redundant message in this guide, but I can't stress enough that you need to know your case and the supporting law. Think about what the opposition will argue at the hearing. Before most hearings you will have an opportunity to file a motion or response first. Then, whoever wrote the initial motion responds one last time. So, you should already have a record of the supporting law on file to point the judge to. Know and cite the cases you need to rely on out loud.

Don't let the opposing lawyer get under your skin. He or she will use the most direct and indirect ways to cheapen your efforts and call you out for using the courts for your own personal crusade. Do not attack the legal system blindly or cling to circumstantial claims of an ongoing conspiracy against you. This will only give your opposition an excuse to write off your arguments as a waste of the court's time.

Richard Nixon once said: "Remember, always give your best. Never get discouraged. Never be petty. Always remember, others may hate you. But those who hate you don't win unless you hate them. And then you destroy yourself."

So, take it from the master, don't let your passion for your case become too personal. Resist the urge to refer to opposing counsel or the opposing party with disparaging names. This is a fight, but it's one where certain courtesies are observed by both sides. As much as it might curdle your blood, you have to respect the people on the other side of the case. It's the only way you can truly understand how they operate and figure out what their next move will be.

Don't be afraid to take a leap of faith now and then, though. Sometimes you have to dance around the system and force your opponent to object. Get your statement out in court, or get a witness to say something critical. Even if the other side can object, sometimes the judge or jury keeps a memo in their subconscious mind about what they saw or heard in the proceedings. No sustained objection can really put the genie all the way back into the bottle. There is a difference between being told to disregard something and actually disregarding it.

Nonetheless, you should fight the objections your opponent will lob at you as well. Try to find a way in which you can get your most incriminating evidence to be considered as to the character of your opposition. You know the strengths of your case, so advocate for those points and positions. Be as succinct and direct as possible. Save the rambling for text filings, and refine your comments for the hearing to a simple but powerful statement of where you stand in the case. You also need to explain why you should prevail under the facts as they are reported on the record and the precedent law that sets the standard for your type of claims.

There are a ton of parallels between writing a well-researched essay and designing an effective courtroom speech. You tell the judge where the case is first, leading up to where it is now. Then you tell the judge where the case is going next. Wrapping it up for the judge or jury means effectively proving that the direction the case will go is bound to favor you. The law supports you, the evidence supports you, and you are _not_ the average pro-se "fool." Force your audience to take you seriously, and always keep your main focus in mind.

Take it one hearing at a time. Don't panic. The case will not develop overnight. Be prepared, but don't be full of useless information that will only clutter the proceedings. If you have a record of the legal argument already on the record before the hearing, just point to lines in those documents during your presentation in court.

Overcome your fear of public speaking and look presentable and professional when you appear in person. If you appear telephonically, be damn sure you have a rock solid phone connection. Even if you feel you are light years ahead of where anyone would expect a pro-se party to be, don't be smug about it. Patiently lay out the record and the legal basis for your claim, counterclaim, or defense. Most cases (under the supervision of fair judges) are won on the Supreme Court and appeals court law, the expert or eye witness(es), the most compelling evidence, and the most patient and humble approach you can muster to building your case.

Ask for witnesses on the stand to verify your exhibits in open court whenever possible. Ask to approach the witness with the exhibit, and ask if he or she recognizes it. Then ask whatever questions you need to. Then announce in open court that the record should show that the witness swore to the authenticity of exhibit such and such. Even against an intolerable judge who tries to limit whatever you do in court and scold you at every turn for representing yourself, you need to get your facts and supporting documentation on the record. You need a roadmap for appeal.

Take deep breaths and stay hydrated when you are speaking. There will be a record of the proceedings, and most courts will allow you to order official court sanctioned audio recordings for a small fee. If the case is important enough, and if it tells an important enough story, you will want these recordings to show how passionate you were about proving your facts. You don't want the tapes to reveal you mumbled the whole time, either. Try not to sound like you are reading something even if you have to write down your remarks. If you are in open court, make eye contact with the judge and/or jury.

The worst thing you can do is fail to listen to the judge's direction of the proceedings. Don't ever talk over a judge. If he or she interrupts you, listen for silence before you respond. Respect goes a long way, even when a judge seems to be purposely trying to ruin your day.

CHAPTER SIX:

Presenting Your Evidence Properly

What you might consider evidence of your claims may not actually be admissible in court. It is crucial to understand The Rules of Evidence for your particular venue and jurisdiction. Evidence is typically packaged within testimony or as physical or written exhibits. Even if you feel that certain information, objects, or personal narratives need to be presented to the judge, the complicated constraints of the judicial system don't allow you as much freedom as you might want to tell your side of the story.

For witnesses in particular, their version of events has to be based on what they personally know and not on what anyone else told them or shared with them. This is not to say a witness can't talk about a conversation they had with someone else. A problem only arises when that conversation is being represented as a statement of fact that only the other person in the conversation can possibly know. Before you present witnesses, you should thoroughly research the "hearsay" principal and make sure what they have to offer is relevant to your case.

Any time you have written material or communications you have to present as evidence, there must be an authentication process. Official records can be faked, so it is important to get what's called a "supporting affidavit" from an authority at the agency or company the records came from. Likewise, you need affidavits from the actual parties who received and/or sent certain written communication that is important to proving your case. When it comes to electronic communication, it also helps to have an expert who can verify all the information that proves the message came from a certain party. Every email and electronic message has certain signature features that a technician can make sense of, from the IP address that pinpoints the location a message is sent from to the schematics that show what service provider and network the sender uses.

Your own affidavits are also important to your case, especially because you typically won't have someone to ask you questions if you take the stand. Affidavits are simply statements of fact, typically numbered and including a notary stamp that shows you swear what is contained within the document is absolutely true to the best of your knowledge. Writing an affidavit can be difficult for people who are used to just telling their story in plain English. An affidavit is not an informal narrative of events. It is an official record of the facts that you can attest to, and it must be written and formatted in the correct manner for it to be admissible in a court of law. Exhibits should always be accompanied by affidavits that authenticate them, and you should also always have exhibits whenever possible to back up the statements you make in affidavits.

One of my worst mistakes in representing myself in the early days of the Xyience case involved my failure to authenticate exhibits. I knew nothing about the process of writing affidavits at the start of that harrowing experience, and that only complicated my case and confused the judge. As I became more familiar with the nuances of the legal process, I gathered affidavits from multiple witnesses to bolster my position. I presented my own affidavit with nearly every motion I put before the court once I realized the importance of such documents.

My personal struggles in multiple courts across the country put me up against a variety of different attorneys. Sometimes a whole legal team would be going up against me, even though I never went to any formal law school. I even found myself fighting for justice against a Harvard educated attorney in federal court. Though I often found myself frustrated and annoyed by some of their legal tactics, I tried to learn as much as I could from the documents and exhibits presented by these attorneys.

Pablo Picasso once said, "Good artists copy. Great artists steal." Picasso did not mean to say that the key to his success was passing off works of other great artists as his own. He used the word "steal" a bit loosely, and if you look at his paintings it is easy to see how he stole the very essence of the subjects he painted. He did not simply copy their expressions and mannerisms. He also studied other artists and used some of their techniques to add to his own basic understanding of creating great art.

The Picasso principle easily translates to writing. It is said that fact is stranger than fiction, and countless fictional tales would not even be conceivable if even more outlandish things did not happen in real life. Most writers learn early on that you should write about what you know, and it is hard to find any fiction writer out there who does not include parts of his own life experiences in his or her work.

Just as a fictional writer uses slightly-altered non-fiction to shape a novel or a short story, you can use the opposing side's paperwork to formulate your own. You don't want to simply copy all the nuances used by your adversary, but you can learn a great deal about formatting and legalese from closely studying the work of lawyers who graduated from prestigious schools and then garnered far more real life legal experience than you can even dream of acquiring as a pro-se party. If you don't have a phenomenal lawyer on the other side of your case, you can turn to other similar cases championed by legal legends. If there is an appeals court case that is relevant, acquiring the representative documents can be one of the best ways to assemble what you need. Try to pick a case that turned out to be successful whenever possible. Look at how exhibits were presented, how affidavits were written and formatted, and how the attorney who won the case framed the evidence in support of his or her claims.

There is admissibility on one hand, and there is relevance on the other hand. It may help you as you formulate evidence to go back and study the kinds of objections that can be raised in court. Relevance is one of the most commonly used reasons to object. To be relevant, the evidence presented must be directly linked to trying to prove or disprove a legal argument or facts crucial to the outcome of the case.

Rule 401 of the Federal Rules of evidence outlines that evidence is relevant if it has the "tendency to make the existence of any fact that is of consequence to the determination of the action more probable or less probable than it would be without the evidence."

Most evidence will be submitted through pre-trial paperwork, but sometimes that's not possible. You may need to refer to evidence or introduce evidence at trial or at an evidentiary hearing. There is typically a process to follow in order to call the court's attention to the specific exhibit.

First, address the judge with something to the effect of, "Your Honor, I would like to present this item for identification as plaintiff's (or defendant's) exhibit 1 (or another number)." You may then be required to show the exhibit to the opposing counsel if he does not already have a copy readily available, and the judge will ask if there are any objections. Typically this procedure is followed when you seek to question a witness about the exhibit. If there are no objections you can present the item to the witness and ask if he or she recognizes it. You might also ask the witness to read some of the wording that is pertinent if it is a document. If the item is a physical object, ask the witness to describe the characteristics of the exhibit. Further questions will be defined by how the exhibit is related to the case and why it is important for the court to consider it in light of the claim.

The best possible evidence you can present in a civil case is often what your opposition is forced to volunteer through interrogatories and/or discovery. Before a civil trial ensues, both parties can engage in the discovery process to force the other side to volunteer facts and evidence that may be relevant to the proceedings. This can include deposing parties before they provide testimony in open court. Interrogatories are formal written questions presented to the opposing party that must be answered under oath (by affidavit). Again, each jurisdiction is different. The Federal Rules of Procedure in the United States allow 25 interrogatories for each party.

The entire discovery process also allows for demanding certain physical evidence from the other party, and refusals to surrender that evidence can lead to court ordered sanctions. Cases are often won or lost in this stage of legal wrangling.

Using a wrongful termination case example, think of a person who knows he has no blemishes on his employment record and gets fired anyway. The plaintiff would request all disciplinary records through discovery, formulate interrogatories which inquire about his exemplary job performance, and ask to depose fellow workers who know about his solid work history in the position he lost unfairly.

Many cases will never go to trial if the risks become too much for one party to bear. Building an incredible wall of evidence is crucial to inspiring settlement before a trial. If you use the discovery process to arm yourself with a mountain of proof, most opposing lawyers will advise their client that a trial is pointless. If you want to negotiate from a position of power, assemble your evidence by using all the discovery tools you have available to you. Get as much as possible on the record before a trial date is even set.

Even in cases where the evidence is overwhelming in your favor, your adversary might still be stubborn enough to take the case to trial. If the opposition is not smart enough to see the writing on the wall or thinks that drawing the process out over time will make you quit, file a motion for summary judgment. Include all the relevant evidence, legal precedents, and pertinent details that prove the case does not need to go to trial. If your evidence is in line, one formal motion and hearing could decide the issue. A so-called "Motion for Summary Judgment" gives you a favorable judgment without the case ever going to trial if a judge chooses to agree with your argument and acknowledge your evidence.

Understanding what constitutes evidence, how to present valid evidence, and how to use it to your advantage is absolutely necessary to successfully representing yourself in court. Memorize your jurisdiction's rules and procedures and build your wall of evidence carefully and artfully. Remind your opposition whenever possible about how much evidence you have and how foolish it is for them to ignore it all and keep going. Nine times out of ten, an opposing attorney will forget you are at a disadvantage in representing yourself if all the evidence supports your legal argument and you know how to force judges to confront it.

CHAPTER SEVEN:

Outworking the Opposition

It is rare for an attorney to have just one case to work on at any given time. Most practicing lawyers have a variety of litigation responsibilities to handle at the same time. This is a difference you can capitalize on if you have enough time to devote to your own legal efforts.

Another important advantage you have is that most attorneys are not that emotionally involved in the cases they work on. On the other hand, you have all the passion in the world for your case. You are always personally invested, and you won't look at working on your case as simply a manner of earning a paycheck.

Unfortunately, there's a huge downside to counteract the upside of this benefit of representing yourself. Typically, you will never see any financial benefit at all unless you win your case. Meanwhile, the opposing attorney usually gets paid an obscene hourly wage even if he or she loses the case. The legal system is only a get-rich-quick plan if you're a bigshot paid lawyer, so you aren't going to make a ton of money in a flash with your case.

Under these circumstances it makes sense to do everything in your power to cost your opponent more legal fees. Being in the bankruptcy case for Xyience allowed me to see multiple legal billing statements for all the attorneys involved. Hundreds of thousands of dollars were devoted to my case alone. I never paid out a dime in judgment, so even if I can't claim a complete victory in the case I can still say my opponent wasted a ton of money trying to silence me and didn't recover any of it from me. I also am not forbidden to write about the Xyience case, so I didn't really lose at all. I just didn't win as big as I could have.

Eventually it will be the proceeds from writing about the case that will pay the judgment I failed to obtain through the courts for the innocent shareholders victimized by the billionaire brothers who drove Xyience into the ground in order to gain complete control of it for themselves. Just because I did not give up in the face of impossible odds and did actually gain a few victories along the way, the story behind the case could generate millions if it starts out with a best-selling book and transitions into a feature film.

Everyone loves an unknown underdog who makes the kind of progress nobody expects him to against a supremely powerful enemy.

Thanks to my hard work fighting back in the Xyience case and chronicling the whole matter on multiple Web-sites and forums, I managed to generate some serious online buzz. Experts and casual observers were paying attention, and every now and then I still stumble on an insightful comment or two left by people who remember the stand I took:

http://themmacommunity.com/threads/seems-a-4th-class-action-was-filed-against-the-ufc-shits-getting-real.589/page-2 (third post down)

Outside of writing commentary on the litigation, I also wrote a number of emails to the attorneys involved and the people they represented. I also called company representatives on the phone trying to find out more information or just trying to let them know I was looking into their activities. Eventually, my adversaries found a way (A.K.A. a restraining order) to prevent me from contacting them in any manner other than snail mail, but not before they spent thousands of dollars in legal fees just for the amount of time it took for paid attorneys to review my communications.

I also managed to "hack" into Xyience's mainframe during the case. This took no specific computer skills at all, because an insider at the company provided me the instructions on how to access the system and what to enter for a login ID and password. I reviewed thousands of documents and had access to everyone's email. I could even watch the company's surveillance cameras at all times of the day and night. Before I could really capitalize on this advantage, there was a court hearing in which I had to admit what I'd done on the stand.

It didn't take long for my loophole for access to close after my confession. The same hearing allowed me the opportunity to question a company executive. The resulting testimony revealed that the company spent tens of thousands of dollars just trying to figure out how I was getting all my damning information. I kept feeding bits and pieces of what I found to the opposing lawyers as proof of shady business going on behind the scenes. Xyience had the offices swept for bugs and hidden cameras, hired a computer firm to review and alter their security settings, held multiple official company meetings with the law firm overseeing the case, and expended thousands of dollars in legal fees just to make sure a judge hit me with a restraining order. I could see them all panic from the inside thanks to my loyal sources.

The point is: lawyers and complicated litigation are expensive. The lawyers opposing you will probably not be paid by billionaires like my adversaries were, though. Some of the costs associated with opposing the case I built inside and outside of court would have crippled any individual or entity with a smaller bank account. The best I could hope for was serious annoyance, which I'm confident I accomplished. If you can think of enough ways to cost the other party an overbearing amount of legal fees (or other financial losses), you might even end up winning by default. They will tap out rather than allow the bleeding to continue.

Another legal opponent of mine was so intimidated by a counterclaim I filed against her that she actually declared personal bankruptcy to avoid having to pay a judgment. She stiffed the attorney who drafted the initial bogus case against me as well. Unfortunately, it's very difficult to prove someone is engaging in bankruptcy fraud or stop the bankruptcy process from proceeding:

http://www.docstoc.com/docs/434271/Motion-To-Suspend-Xyience-Bankruptcy-Motion-For-Summary-Judgment

Still, formulating and publishing crucial court documents packed with evidence can at least make your opposition think long and hard about keeping up the fight against you. The above link is an example of a document that the judge did nothing about, but the public read voraciously. It is the top-viewed document I have available on docstoc.com, mainly because it was picked up by so many other media outlets other than my own.

You will have to do your best to build your own case in the time you have available. If you have a day job that you can't take a break from, you'll likely have to suffer through some long nights. Doing research and formulating the right paperwork can take hours, and on top of this you may have to make a variety of phone calls and/or set up formal face-to-face meetings with potential witnesses.

Nobody said being your own lawyer would be easy. It's a nightmare Stephen King could have created a best-selling novel about if he'd ever gone through it himself.

King's actual life story is a phenomenal example of perseverance and determination. If you read anything about his background, you understand why so much of his work contains the common themes of Maine, laundries and so much mind-numbing horror. King developed his own unique voice through relaying his own life experiences and careful and constant study of the fictional works he enjoyed reading the most. He used his writing to show his appreciation for all the old-school horror films and comic books he devoured as a kid, but he always had his own unique twist on things. As an adult, King worked at a laundry operation while writing for smut magazines at night. Somewhere along the way a small fan base blossomed into multiple best-selling novels, too many movies to name here, and a place in literary history as one of the most compelling fiction writers of our age.

The point is, King worked very hard at the beginning, like most successful people have to do to make it to the top. He had a day job just like you. If you want to have success in a climate where the odds are stacked against you before you start, persistence is a virtue. King tells a story in *"On Writing"* about nailing a railroad spike to his wall and attaching all his rejection letters from potential publishers to it. He put that spike to the test before he became famous, and it took plenty of rejection to find a few people who said yes. He knew early in his budding career that the law of averages leaned heavily in his favor. Practice made perfect, and eventually King managed to retire the spike and carry his talent to super stardom.

A self-represented party has to accumulate court experience, even if it's negative, in order to really understand how it all works. During the Xyience case, I tripped all over myself trying to make sense of the process. The first hearings were uncomfortable and nerve wracking, but by the end I felt very at home in the actual courthouse. At the start of the case, I could relate to the following observation made by Comedian Jim Gaffigan:

http://media.kism.com/Comedian_Jim_Gaffigan_on_Legal_Documents.mp3

Don't be intimidated by the difficulty of swimming upstream in a biased system. If you run into a roadblock in how to proceed, you might turn to a Web-site that answers legal questions or an official legal aid program. Sometimes there will be a fee involved, but don't worry if you can't afford that route. Try to find a free legal forum that can serve the same purpose. Better yet, contact a number of attorneys in your jurisdiction as a person who might want to hire them. One or more of them will probably call you back or email you about the case, and you might be able to get them to answer your questions without having to pay a dime.

There are also a variety of unconventional legal tactics you can use that most lawyers would never resort to. You can act as your own private investigator in many cases, uncovering on or off-the-record background information that could help your case. During the Xyience saga, I actually had a number of people who sought me out to tell me the company's horror stories. That led me to other people who I could call or email to question personally. Some of these people sent me supporting documentation or other evidence I could use in the case.

Believe it or not, my best weapon against my adversary turned out to be a phone.

Even if you can't use what you find in court, you can publish what you find (read the next chapter for more on this subject). You can also use any off-the-record material to further your investigation. You don't always have to let the other side know how you obtained certain information, and if it is incriminating or damaging enough you could still inspire a settlement by leveraging what you find before you make any attempt to introduce it as evidence in court.

Sometimes lawyers use paperwork like a weapon. They will send one phone book of material after another to you in the hopes that you will take one look at it all and think you will never have a chance at winning. Do not get discouraged. Read it all. Pick out everything you can that is inconsistent. Use whatever errors you find against the lawyer(s) who drafted the material. Call out the opposition in open court for wasting the court's time with meaningless drivel if that's what it all really amounts to.

During the Xyience case, the opposition included over a hundred pages of material from Lucille's federal case that had nothing to do with the proceedings. I suggested in open court that if he wanted to try that case he should call the counsel for that plaintiff and volunteer his time to that effort. I outlined all the reasons why that material had no place on the record of the Xyience case and should not be considered as evidence of any valid legal argument. I further argued that the attorney should face sanctions for cluttering the docket with useless information. I even added that all the copies of the associated documents represented a colossal waste of trees.

You have to have that much confidence in your case to win sometimes. The key is to know everything there is to know, because the opposition will have no answer to a smart and slick pro-se defense. Make phone calls. Talk to whoever you can who knows anything about the matter. Make official legal demands for documentation. Sometimes the PACER system alone can give you a number of decent leads, especially if you find your opponent has a record of civil and/or criminal litigation a mile long. You can find phone numbers and contact information for key witnesses all over PACER. During the early stages of the Xyience case an attorney I contacted who previously worked with the company's founder gave me the best background information to show the guy was a classic con artist.

Much of what you find won't be admissible or relevant in court, but you can often use the information to get under an opponent's skin in direct communications. In an important case where you are also publishing information about your journey, it will be these exchanges that generate the most reader interest. Liars do not like to be confronted about their lies, and a little smug confidence in your approach to exposing them works every time. They'll typically bite back, and you'll know you have the ability to irritate them.

No matter how little progress you feel you are making, if you work hard enough to learn the laws of the land and the pomp and circumstance of giving speeches in open court, you will have an excellent record for appeal. If a local judge has it out for you or wants to ignore the law, appeal the case. This is where outworking your opposition is absolutely essential. It's a game changer. You really need to constantly educate yourself on the prevailing Supreme Court law on your case's topic of interest and the type of claim you are bringing and/or facing. Research all the appeals cases you can find with similar scenarios unfolding in those cases that would benefit your claim being decided in the same vein.

You don't have to be perfect, but your paperwork shouldn't be sloppy, either. Again, don't be afraid to look to the experts in this regard. Writing great legal documentation is all about reading and creating your own personalized version of the best legal material you can find that is similar enough to what you ultimately want to produce. From format to content, nothing is better to guide you in your legal writing than the same type of motion or filing that an impeccably-trained attorney fighting for the right side of your particular issue wrote on a landmark case.

Though lawyering might seem on TV like it hinges on what happens inside the courtroom, most cases are actually won on paper long before a trial is even scheduled. The paperwork is also one of the most complicated aspects of representing yourself. Some paperwork can be essential to pressing your case and keeping your opponents working. If you have limited income, a "motion to proceed informa pauperis" could help you go through the entire case without having to pay any filing fees that normally apply. As mentioned earlier, a summary judgment motion could end the case before trial. A carefully crafted affidavit could also contain enough relevant evidence to blow your opposition out of the water.

There is a time in every man or woman's life when a situation calls for a fight. Giving up is not an option. Anyone hit with a serious lawsuit knows the angst and endless worry that comes from imagining how your life would change if you lost. Some might be motivated to win by this factor alone, but for most it is not enough. The ultimate goal has to also encompass a more positive outcome to drive for. This is where working harder than your adversary is crucial.

My own case against Xyience, Incorporated went from the district court level in Las Vegas to Federal Bankruptcy Court. During much of the six-plus-year period the case proceeded, it seemed like an inchworm trying to reach the end of a marathon. The process is often the worst part of representing yourself. It's slow, unwieldy and generally obstinate about amateurs trying to navigate it. The effort I put into the paperwork and the time spent on research felt like a part time job at the busiest times, but the whole fiasco taught me some valuable lessons about the law.

I finally began to understand why my editors would always get anxious and nervous when I was working on a controversial subject as a small town newspaper reporter. They would always warn me the paper could get sued when I wanted to write about a major scandal. Fighting the Xyience case turned out to be crucial to my development as an independent writer. I wanted to make sure the threat of legal action would never muzzle me again when I had a worthy investigative report to pursue. By the end of the Xyience case I was ready for the next scumbag who would rather bury the truth than confront it.

I eventually learned to embrace the grind of preparing for hearings and writing stacks of my own filings in response to my adversaries. The reality is, standing up and fighting back in the Xyience lawsuit likely saved me more headaches from The Eppley vs.

Iacovelli case I mentioned in Chapter Two of this book. I was named in injunction requests and resulting orders that were part of Dr. Eppley's case, but not as a defendant.

Dr. Barry Eppley, an Indianapolis plastic surgeon, sued a former patient named Lucille Iacovelli before I could even start writing a book I was planning to put together about her unique and intriguing case. This happened at a time when the Xyience case was still puttering through bankruptcy:

http://www.dmlp.org/threats/eppley-v-iacovelli

Lucille Iacovelli was a patient of Eppley's who blamed him for destroying her facial structure and degrading her quality of life in the process. She complained of ringing in the ears and trouble talking, eating, breathing, and aspirating fluids in the wake of the surgery Eppley performed on her in Indianapolis. Her ordeal became a lifetime battle, and she actually appeared on an HBO documentary entitled *"Plastic Disasters."* She never sued Eppley for malpractice, because she was discouraged by the cost of an expert witness and the other outlandish legal fees that pressing such a case would entail.

Instead, Eppley actually sued Lucille in March, 2009 after her online posting about her horrible experience and her activism against plastic surgery in general became too costly for his ongoing plastic surgery business to bear. He explained at one point in the proceedings that he had to spend two to three thousand dollars a month on "reputation management."

It was years since the surgery in question, and Eppley never sued the people involved in the HBO documentary. Lucille didn't have much more than disability income, so it wasn't about getting her money. Like most evil in this world we live in, all you have to do is follow the money to understand Eppley's Modus Operandi.

Customers were reading awful things about him online, and people who initially wanted surgery decided against it after reading what Lucille wrote. Even if it was the truth, Eppley would not prosper if people kept reading about it, so he sought out to eliminate the source. Sadly, he succeeded.

Lucille killed herself in August of 2010, and the events leading up to her suicide will be the subject of a novel based on a true story I plan to write in the next few years. She faced impossible odds and diabolical enemies in her final struggle to regain her freedom. Eppley kept right on suing her estate after her death. His slick lawyers (including the one with the dunce hat on his head earlier in the book) were even able to get Lucille's estranged sister (who cooperated and conspired with Eppley while her sister was alive) to be the official representative for her estate. Check out http://www.arlenemulleysucks.com to learn more about a woman who could be considered the living definition of the term "evil sister."

A pathologist I consulted about Lucille's story later told me that the whole litigation probably didn't even cost the doctor himself a dime. This expert explained to me that the case would have been something paid for by just about any doctor's own practice/malpractice insurance, especially if he could prove that silencing the squeaky wheel was crucial to the bottom line of his lucrative business. All he had to do was accuse her of lying. The judge in the case even let him be his own expert witness on the procedure he allegedly performed in a substandard and sloppy manner.

This is the same kind of fouled-up system you might end up facing, and just like me you might not believe such corruption can be possible. Trust me, it is more than possible. It's the norm in too many jurisdictions where too many judges have more power than any one person should possess.

I thought the cronyism and corruption in the Xyience case was bad, but then I became involved in Lucille's case. Though I was not a defendant, the judge subjected me to a restraining order forbidding me from writing a single word about the operation Eppley performed on Lucille. Judge Sarah Evans Barker didn't even allow me to publish a single word about the Eppley case or place the actual case documents on third-part hosting sites like docstoc. I defied her orders until she shut all my pertinent Web-sites down. The most popular site (www.judgegod.com) portrayed the judge as the Queen of Hearts from Lewis Carroll's Alice in Wonderland and featured a picture of an actual kangaroo with the Judge Sarah Evans Barker's head on it:

A really difficult situation unfolded before I could blink in the Eppley case. I had no genuine opportunity to really represent myself in the case, and I knew what Lucille was in store for thanks to my own legal experience. I knew she could not physically handle appearing by telephone, but I encouraged her to try it for the first hearing. She received approval to appear with me on a conference line for that first hearing. I had little opportunity to speak for myself or Lucille on the call. She could barely breathe, let alone talk. The biased judge ruled that Lucille would have to appear in person from that moment on or not appear at all. It was basically the same thing that happened to me the first time I appeared in person in Las Vegas, but this time we were both trying to participate over the phone. This refusal to allow Lucille to appear in any meaningful fashion at the hearings alienated her and I from the process from day one. The only way we could find out what really went on at hearings would be to order transcripts.

Already, Lucille felt like a victim all over again, and there was no way possible to win the case as far as she was concerned. This incredible woman derived much of her strength from at least being able to write about her ordeal and share her photos, videos and daily struggle to cope. Judge Sarah Evans Barker took her right of expression away from Lucille without any semblance of due process or respect for her side of the story.

The only responsible thing to do in light of Barker's blatant disrespect of the law also happened to be technically illegal.

I wrote every single pleading and piece of paperwork for Lucille's case, motivated purely by a desire to right a serious wrong. There was no potential to make money by defending Lucille. She couldn't pay me, and I wouldn't stand for payment anyway. She never filed any counterclaims and didn't want Eppley's money. A "practicing without a license" charge would be tough to apply to me if I wasn't collecting any fees, so I did also have that factor in my favor. Still, Eppley's attorneys did their best to nail me on that when I finally admitted to writing everything for Lucille after she passed away.

Though I defied multiple orders and raised as much Hell about the whole thing as I possibly could, my ultimate tab in the case amounted to less than $1,000 in filing fees and contempt charges. I will never pay any amount to that court. I consider every order of Judge Barker's to be unconstitutional, and I have all the evidence and law to support that claim should there be any future attempt to collect those fees.

The judge really screwed Lucille over by not allowing her to truly confront her accuser. She had no opportunity to cross examine Dr. Eppley when he provided his "expert" witness testimony. At that point, Eppley and his attorneys were in complete control. The same judge denied me a voice in the case to fight against having my own words suppressed by Eppley even before I published anything about his operation on Lucille.

Due to my limited legal experience and familiarity with the process, I really felt as if Lucille's case could be won in any other scenario aside from the one we found ourselves in. Unfortunately, money is power in the court process. Bad things happen to good people every day in court, and it's usually because they can't afford adequate representation. This was a case where I think even the best representation money could buy would have no chance to win in front of that judge. I just wanted to make sure Lucille had the best representative possible so her legacy could be protected, and I truly believed her story had real potential to help countless victims struggling with the results of their own botched surgeries.

I took Lucille's case all the way to the 7th Circuit Court of Appeals only to find out how infallible federal judges really are. The Supreme Court provided an incredibly powerful framework of protections that can be found in their most significant issues tackling areas of free speech. Our nation is built on the principal idea of declaring ourselves free from royal and tyrannical repression, so being freely allowed to criticize public officials is crucial to the smooth running of the political system as well as the justice system even today. Judge Barker was a public official who put herself above established Supreme Court Law. The 7th Circuit acted like there was nothing they could do to stop her.

"There exists a profound national commitment to the principle that debate on public issues should be uninhibited, robust, and wide-open, and that it may well include vehement, caustic, and sometimes unpleasantly sharp attacks on government and public officials," wrote William J. Brennan, Jr., Associate Justice of the Supreme Court of the United States in the case of *New York Times Co. v. Sullivan*, which the court decided in 1964.

I endured all the negative developments that unfolded in both my cases due to sheer corruption, bias, and the system being geared toward practicing attorneys. I fought on for the record, knowing I would lose but still hang on to the greater story I could not ultimately be prevented from telling. I also knew at least the case could make the rounds in the media and someone might look it up and benefit from all the research I did and the law I cited to support Lucille's position. The outcome of any final order signed by Judge Barker would never really prevent me from writing Lucille's story. On the contrary, enduring the heart-wrenching drama and stress associated with that legal fight only inspired me more to get the story into print. At this point it is just a matter of putting the time into that effort before it can be released. It's the kind of story that writes itself.

At this point, I would welcome Eppley to take a legal shot at me whenever I do put Lucille's story into a manuscript and publish it. I honestly want him to sue me and see how it goes against someone who can actually fight back in a court of law. It would be a much fairer fight than going after a frail old woman like Lucille, even if he manages to get another sympathetic judge who is willing to ignore established law to support his position.

Even though Lucille and I both lost a great deal in the fight, the story is not over and the book is by no means closed on this case. An official companion site for the book I plan to write will also detail the nuances of the real case and give readers a better idea of why such a book had to be written in the first place. Judge Barker, Dr. Eppley, and Attorney Todd Richardson will all probably want to sue me if I can manage to adequately capture and describe their diabolical behavior in the final accounting of the life and times of Lucille Iacovelli.

The value truly has to be intrinsic for you to even bother to involve yourself in the impossible task of teaching yourself how to be a lawyer to tackle a complicated case. You can never expect to win as much as you may hope to. Sometimes it just doesn't matter how hard you work to win your case, because the game is rigged. You have to have your own game in mind to really get anything out of all the legal fighting.

Outworking your opposition does not stop when the case does if you end up losing the good fight. If you truly want and need justice, you have to seek it through multiple channels. If there are any honest lawyers out there, they will tell you a court room is often the last place on earth a person should go to find real justice. Talk to a victim like Lucille, and chances are you will discover exactly what she told me one day about malpractice lawsuits:

"I don't want a million dollars from Eppley or any money really," Lucille said. "What I really want more than anything else is what every victim of negligence or malpractice wants: an apology. The sad thing is, that almost never happens."

Sometimes winning in such a corrupt process isn't even satisfying. Legal cases often end in settlements, and this could mean a doctor like Eppley ultimately goes unpunished in a malpractice or negligence situation he settles. All he has to do is throw money at the problem. Celebrities, successful businessmen and wealthy individuals of all stripes also use lawyers and quiet settlements to avoid facing the consequences for their worst transgressions. Most situations in which a party receives a settlement, there is specific language forbidding the public discussion of any valid details. So, the offending party gets away with the wrongdoing and makes sure you can never name and shame him in the future. He or she can then repeat the bad behavior and the same process of silencing the innocent victims that behavior unfairly targets.

The sheer length of the process makes settlements the preferred method of ending a case, so hanging on for an actual judgment might not seem possible for many pro-se parties. Even with a judgment, an offender can still find a way to victimize someone else down the line. So, even winning isn't everything, as the saying goes. Often the more important thing is doing everything in your power to stop others from suffering the same fate you did at the hands of the same offender. That takes engaging the court of public opinion and exposing your adversary's misdeeds to a wider audience than a judge or jury.

One of my favorite quirky sayings is "sunlight is the best disinfectant." Exposing the ills of your adversary and laying out their methodology and shady habits for everyone to see could be the key to making sure your experience helps others steer clear of danger.

Still, there is value in the court fight, especially if you find yourself in a struggle regular, everyday people can relate to. If you can inspire one person with your effort, it might be worth it to try. At the very least, you are costing your foe money by refusing to give in and not allowing yourself to be steamrolled. There is another important saying you should always keep in mind when things are not going your way in the legal process: "What doesn't kill you makes you stronger."

The mayhem and madness I experienced as my own lawyer during the whole process infuriated me enough to become ultra-aggressive. As I mentioned earlier, during my pursuit of the real story behind the Fertitta family's rise to fame and fortune in Las Vegas, people always wanted to know if I was afraid I was "gonna get whacked." By the time the final check I received in the case arrived in my mailbox, my adversaries seemed to be far more intimidated by me than I was by them. One of their lawyers even claimed my reporting was causing his clients incredible difficulties with the state gaming authorities. I reminded that attorney that if I wrote anything that was untrue about his clients, they could sue me and prove it.

The trouble I caused the Fertittas with the gaming authorities had nothing to do with any misrepresented statements or false accusations I made in my reporting. Their real problems arose when I began to reveal the shady legal history behind the business operations of Fertitta Enterprises, a family holding and investments company. I exposed actual legal documents, detailing (and in one case diagramming) a shady loan scheme the Fertittas orchestrated:

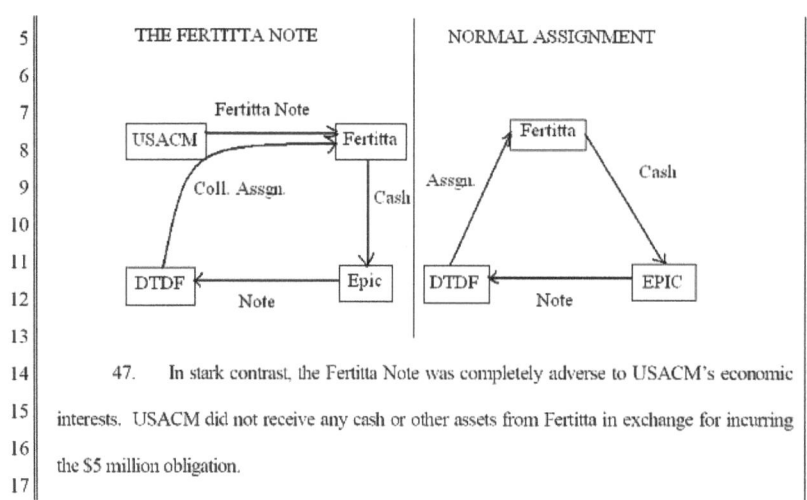

47.   In stark contrast, the Fertitta Note was completely adverse to USACM's economic interests. USACM did not receive any cash or other assets from Fertitta in exchange for incurring the $5 million obligation.

The company involved in loaning money to the Fertittas in the above scheme ended up being the subject of a major federal investigation. One officer of the company served prison time for his role in questionable loan packages:

http://www.fbi.gov/lasvegas/press-releases/2010/lv040910.htm

The Fertittas obviously have better lawyers.

Finding out that I caused them to sweat a few more bullets in front of the gaming authorities made my day when I heard it in open court. Suddenly here was my powerful adversary crying foul and claiming my efforts were leading to serious trouble for their most lucrative business interests. I was glad to hear it, because people should be taking a closer look at their history and asking more serious questions about why they keep getting away with screwing people over.

My theory is people like that start small, get away with something petty and keep building and building in their scheming as long as they don't get caught or pay any consequences. Each new scheme becomes bigger than the last, more intricate and hidden, more dangerous to society as a whole if the behavior persists. Only fantastic lawyers and the greased wheels of countless political and charitable donations saved the Fertittas from being overwhelmed by their corrupt past. The gaming commission can ask questions and make the Fertittas uncomfortable, but they can never evict the family from running their casino business in Vegas. It would take something incredibly big and bad to run that family out of town. Still, the least I can do is expose all the reasons they still don't deserve to have a gaming license in the first place.

Where most people would be intimidated by that power standing on the opposite side of a legal matter against you, I found a way to make it a David vs. Goliath situation. I used the powerful beast's own hefty weight against itself. The blogger's "pen" really was mightier than the legal "sword" in this case. It was the best legal education I could ask for.

I guarantee that you will also learn valuable life skills if you choose to represent yourself. If there is a bigger picture involved in your case and other people can learn from your predicament, that's all the more reason to keep fighting. The harder you work, the closer you will get to making some kind of difference in the world that truly matters, whether you win your case or not. All you have to do is get noticed for the way you fight and the reasons why you fight.

One of the best ways to make sure that representing yourself doesn't end up as a total loss is to make your story more accessible to the masses. You don't have to write a novel like I plan to. Just a simple blog will do. Thankfully, there is an ever-expanding array of platforms where you can share your story with millions of people all over the world. That's just what I did, and I will tell you how it worked in my favor in the next chapter.

CHAPTER EIGHT:

Publicizing Your Position or Plight

If you have any writing skills at all or know someone who does, the story you tell outside of court paperwork might actually be more effective than anything you formally submit to any judge or jury.

Whatever your position is in a particular case, you can utilize the mainstream media or create your own social marketing campaign to share it with the masses. If your story and your case are interesting and intriguing enough to warrant any media attention, it could be go downhill quickly for your opposition.

My response to the Xyience case against me included keeping my writing up on the case and the company as long as I could without running afoul of the system. Some of my postings had to be taken down due to the early court rulings, but I left the comment sections up on all of them. The original piece generated 83 comments, including my own regular contributions to keep the conversation going and respond to accusations against me. If you have time to read all these ramblings, they tell a story of company infighting and sheer panic on the part of some players involved in the fraud I was reporting on.

http://unlimitedfightnews.com/wordpress/xyience-investigative-report-creator-russell-pikes-criminal-tendencies-revealed/

The folks trying to paint the culprits I was writing about as upstanding citizens were the most outspoken in the comments. I could tell there were people from the company bickering back and forth with investors and interested parties.

Even with my limited knowledge of "Search Engine Optimization," I knew that all those comments were making the story easier to find online. The same people who wanted to shut me up were actually helping me get the word out to a wider audience.

I had the advantage of starting with an already established fan base in combat sports, where Xyience was a prominent sponsor of mixed martial arts (MMA) athletes and cornering teams from boxing and MMA. The initial claim against me insisted my work alone caused the company to lose over $25 million in investments. Ultimately this was the lie sold to many burned investors who the billionaire Fertitta brothers could have easily bailed out with a fair offer. Instead, they wrote all Xyience's debt off through bankruptcy after using the supplement and energy drink company as proof that their mixed martial arts league, the Ultimate Fighting Championship, was a strong and financially viable enough company to qualify for a huge credit and financing package. I followed the money, and I hit a nerve.

I had the good fortune of having the facts straight and an ability to dig deeper to find more facts to add to the pile. Instead of weakening my resolve to publish the truth, the lawsuit only made me more inclined to keep reporting and get to the bottom of the lies and fraud. Intimidation gave way to acceptance, and the next stage was a crusade to get my revenge. I set out to expose the Fertittas for all their past transgressions and heartless victimizing of honest, hardworking people. Throughout their history it seemed to me that this family wanted to line their own pockets off the backs of better men than themselves, and they just considered it smart business to screw people over. I didn't care who they knew and how powerful they were. I simply saw an opportunity to put them in their place and expose their corrupt history.

Every now and then, I hear a story like the one someone told me about a guest on Lorenzo Fertitta's private jet asking him a few uncomfortable questions about Xyience. Fertitta's son was within earshot, as pops was flying the boy to a college football tryout as the story goes. Lorenzo found a way to change the subject according to my witness, and it appeared obvious from his reaction that the questions rattled the billionaire.

Sometimes it is those miniscule victories that really lift your spirit when you face such impossible odds of winning in court. They might be all you get if you face people with unlimited resources like I had to.

If your story is not so exciting and dynamic and your case is fairly mundane, it might take a much more creative effort to get people to notice it. As a former newspaper reporter, my training taught me to avoid "becoming part of the story." It's like a cardinal sin for people in the news business. You just don't toot your own horn, but in this case I absolutely had to in order to sustain a counter-offensive.

You don't have to be Ernest Hemingway. Sometimes just a few sentences and pertinent links to supporting documentation can shake the foundation of your opposition if enough people read all that material. Sometimes only a handful of people may need to see the truth for you to gain an advantage in a particular case. Whatever you publish must be backed up by fact, and you must be careful to follow the law whenever you possibly can.

I had some urgent situations where I skirted the law and violated unconstitutional orders, but I would not recommend this approach if you can find a way to avoid it. Use appeals to go after crooked judges before you resort to outright defiance of court orders. I had the advantage of owning a small time and independent combat sports news site (www.fightnewsunlimited.com) rather than an international media conglomerate with endless financial coffers. Contempt fees and court-ordered sanctions in civil cases can actually be applied proportionately to a person's wealth, so being too poor to afford a lawyer was actually a plus for me in this David vs. Goliath scenario.

To keep your opposition anxious and concerned, write as much as you can to expose their worst transgressions. Be sure there are no restrictions on writing about your case, no orders forbidding you from making certain claims, and no chance of you being punished by the courts in any way for speaking out. Contact as many pertinent people as possible. The approach of exposing an adversary in this manner is often called "name and shame," and it's been a part of the American culture for longer than you might realize. Legal punishment in colonial days sometimes called for offenders to have their heads and hands locked in a crude device so their fellow citizens could throw rotten vegetables at them.

These days, "public shaming" with written words alone can also be incredibly cruel and mean instead of serving a genuine and positive purpose, so be very careful. Do not cross the line and bully your opposition, make threats of any kind, or act overly aggressive. Write the truth and break it down in to the simplest terms you can think of. Be creative. Use visual aids like documentary-style videos and illustrations. Study other viral videos and content and copy the methods used to popularize those success stories.

There are plenty of civilized, dignified and easily-accessible ways to provide maximum exposure to your position or plight in a particular legal case. Rather than accost your opponent and throw rancid tomatoes at him, you have to take a more dynamic and inventive approach these days.

Even if a judge does order your content removed from the Internet, they might not be able to facilitate complete destruction of your efforts. The more content you put out there on anonymous forums and in the comment sections of pertinent stories that might be related, the more likely you are to be able to avoid any removal orders. Forums and comment sections are actually more protected than actual articles on Web-sites. The idea is that these areas are not generally seen as places to look to when you want everything you read to be true. These are the sections of sites in which it is expected for people to offer their opinions, which are also more protected than fact-based statements.

Although MySpace seems to become less and less popular as time passes, one of my most potent videos about Lucille Iacovelli's case is still posted there:

http://unlimitedfightnews.com/wordpress/lucille-iacovelli-tribute-video/

I don't know if the reason it still exists has anything to do with MySpace being so out of touch that you can't even contact an administrator through the site itself. What I do know is that if I put it on YouTube, it likely wouldn't survive very long. The doctor who sued Lucille actually trademarked his own name to have some extra leverage when going after critics like Lucille. Unfortunately, the doc's lawyers misrepresented the whole realm of trademark law that prevents a person from trademarking their name to avoid public criticism. If trademarking your name meant nobody could ever say you did anything wrong, every politician in the United States would be lining up to get their own names trademarked. Imagine how boring presidential campaigns would be if that were the case.

The reality is trademark infringement only occurs when you are using the trademark in a way that is "confusingly similar" to the way the trademark holder is using it. So, Lucille would actually have to be using the name to sell plastic surgery services in order to allow the doctor to sue for trademark infringement in a court where there was a totally unbiased judge presiding. Judge Sarah Evans Barker did not seem to grasp—or purposely ignored—the established trademark law that is designed to prevent unfair business practices and protect people from having their business names stolen out from under them or used to sell something that's not their official product or service.

Lucille was not selling anything. She was just describing her own personal experience with the doctor, warning other potential plastic surgery patients to be wary of what doctor they choose and what risks they could face in going under the knife. She should have only been held accountable if her sites looked somewhat similar to the doctor's official site to the extent that people looking for the doctor would find her site and think it was his.

The doctor's lawyers also purposely constructed case documents that flat out tried to prevent my own book about Lucille from seeing the light of day. They did this before a word of that book was actually written and before a single query letter to a potential publisher went out. Preventing "future speech" is very difficult to do under these circumstances in courts where the judges are not overtly biased toward the party seeking to impose such restrictions on another party.

It should be especially difficult to restrict a person's future speech when the lawsuit does not name the person the restrictions target as an actual party to the case. The doc and his lawyers obviously knew I could represent myself and cause them some headaches, so they sued Lucille only and labeled me as a co-conspirator in what they classified as her relentless quest to defame the doctor. They were allowed to include me in a preliminary and permanent injunction even though I was not actually permitted to participate in any meaningful way in the proceedings. This is another reason why I wrote every pleading for Lucille in the case.

News outlets that did cover the case typically took the doctor's side or pointed to Lucille being labeled as having "Body Dysmorphic Disorder." Unfortunately, this affliction known as BDD is also used by doctors to dismiss patients as nuts or delusional. It's an out and an excuse more than an actual condition suffered by those who have legitimate complaints about substandard plastic surgery. It's actually a fairly brilliant idea as much as I hate the fact that it is so pervasive in the industry. After all, what better way to defend your own work than to call the person complaining about it crazy?

The Fox News LA segment I participated in cut out the majority of my interview and didn't even mention the pertinent details of the case or Lucille's accusations against the doctor:

http://www.myfoxla.com/story/18419056/the-truth-behind-plastic-surgery

The one writer who spent the most time trying to research the whole situation relegated her part of his story to the bottom of the piece and really didn't use much of the material he gleaned from interviewing me and reviewing her emails:

http://www.buzzfeed.com/jakerossen/insult-and-injury-inside-the-webs-one-sided-war-on-doctors#.hlwDKyvL3

That writer left me with the impression that he was doing this article all about Lucille's case by itself. I even provided him passwords to copies of all of Lucille's personal blogs that were removed by the doctor, and he did nothing with any of that content at all. I can't say I blame Mr. Rossen. All these traditional media outlets are often overly cautious to avoid the same type of lawsuit that destroyed Lucille's whole outlook on life.

There was no money to gain from Lucille other than monthly disability payments, but her work to expose the doctor and the pitfalls of plastic surgery was worth more than money to her. It was her legacy. Newspapers, magazines, TV stations and major Web-sites all have to try to avoid incurring huge legal fees due to an article that could be subject to a lawsuit.

The above video also includes some snippets of the case documents with precedents that fully explain why this doctor should not have been able to get away with this illicit abuse of the legal system. If Judge Sarah Evans Barker were not so willing to bend over backwards for a person who practiced under the same health care system she served on the board of directors for, she would have followed the law and denied Eppley's claims when confronted with the precedent cases and examples I raised in Lucille's pleadings.

Here is one example from one of my pleadings in Lucille's case explaining why "future speech" or "prior restraint" is typically unconstitutional due to free speech protections:

"

The Supreme Court has several times emphasized that care must be taken to insure that what is restricted is insulting and offensive language, not the communication of offensive ideas. "It is firmly settled that under our Constitution the public expression of ideas may not be prohibited merely because the ideas themselves are offensive to some of their hearers." *Street v. New York*, 394 U.S. 576, 592, 89 S.Ct. 1354, 1366, 22 L.Ed.2d 572 (1969); see *Organization for a Better Austin v. Keefe*, 402 U.S. 415, 419, 91 S.Ct. 1575, 29 L.Ed.2d 1 (1971); *Bachellar v. Maryland*, 397 U.S. 564, 90 S.Ct. 1312, 25 L.Ed.2d 570 (1970).

Even where the audience is so offended by the ideas being expressed that it becomes disorderly and attempts to silence the speaker, it is the duty of the police to attempt to protect the speaker, not to silence his speech if it does not consist of unprotected epithets. *Gooding v. Wilson*, 405 U.S. 518, 527, 92 S.Ct. 1103, 31 L.Ed.2d 408 (1972); *Gregory v. City of Chicago*, 394 U.S. 111, 89 S.Ct. 946, 22 L.Ed.2d 134 (1969); *Cox v. Louisiana*, 379 U.S. 536, 546-48, 85 S.Ct. 453, 13 L.Ed.2d 471 (1965).

"

A particular and somewhat universally applicable case that effectively counters most bogus defamation claims (if you have an impartial judge on your case) is Paul V. Davis, a Supreme Court case from 1976. (http://en.wikipedia.org/wiki/Paul_v._Davis)

"

explained that: "[t]he private litigants' interest in protecting their vanity or their commercial self-interest simply does not qualify as grounds for imposing a prior restraint" (*Procter & Gamble Co. v. Bankers Trust Co.* 78 F.3d 219, 227 (6th Cir. 1996)) and Redress for injury to reputation is not a right protected by the U.S. Constitution, *Paul v. Davis, (1976) 424 U.S. 693, 47 L. Ed. 2d 405, 96 S. Ct. 1155.*

"

Lust like police labeled Edward C. Davis III a shoplifter despite criminal claims being dropped against him, Lucille labeled Eppley as a negligent doctor without a civil judgment or criminal negligence conviction. The cases may deal with different nuances, but they are essentially identical in spirit. Davis and the doctor in Lucille's case both didn't want their names smeared all across the community by those who had poor experiences with them. It is often said that you "cannot prove a negative," which means that most admissible evidence has to show beyond a reasonable doubt that something actionable happened that the claiming party deserves relief for. So, it is not the doctor's charge to provide definitive proof that he never injured Lucille in any way. He must instead prove that she lied or misrepresented the facts of her case and wrote erroneous narratives in her descriptions of his behavior and his medical practice. This doctor had no such proof of Lucille being dishonest beyond his own personal eyewitness testimony, which Judge Barker allowed as an "expert opinion." Even though his insurance was likely paying for the whole case, the doctor didn't even bother to try to find someone independent to review the case files and Lucille's complaints. He simply got up on the stand and testified that he could not have possibly done the kind of damage Lucille accused him of. This was taken as gospel as if this doctor was an impartial witness with no discernible bias.

There is so much of Lucille's case that just cannot be explained here. It is really a diabolical example of how the justice system can truly destroy a person. Readers should no doubt be able to grasp now why I often compared Judge Barker to The Queen of Hearts character in Lewis Carrol's *Alice in Wonderland*. Ironically I discovered another case in which Judge Barker's impartiality was called into question, and the ruling quoted a particular selection from *Alice in Wonderland* featuring the queen's tirade against Alice:

http://www.plainsite.org/dockets/21mu65pxa/indiana-southern-district-court/sexson-v-servaas/?add=1 **(complete ruling)**

Footnote 5:

"Counsels' method of putting allegation before factual inquiry is reminiscent of the trial in Alice in Wonderland:

[T]he White Rabbit blew three blasts on the trumpet, and then unrolled the parchment scroll, and read [the charge] as follows: —

"The Queen of Hearts, she made some tarts, All on a summer day;

The Knave of Hearts, he stole those tarts, And took them quite away!"

"Consider your verdict," the King said to the jury.

"Not yet, not yet!" the Rabbit hastily interrupted. "There's a great deal to come before that!"....

"Give your evidence, said the King; "and don't be nervous, or I'll have you executed on the spot."....

"No, no!" said the Queen. "Sentence first — verdict afterwards."

"Stuff and nonsense!" said Alice loudly. "The idea of having the sentence first!"

"Hold your tongue!" said the Queen, turning purple.

"I won't!" said Alice.

"Off with her head!" the Queen shouted at the top of her voice.

Lewis Carroll, Alice in Wonderland 139-40, 141-42, 157-58 (Mount Vernon: Peter Pauper Press).

Not surprisingly, the barriers for recusing a federal judge from any case are very difficult to get around. You basically have to get the judge to admit out loud that he or she doesn't like you and will never rule in your favor.

Most judges actually recuse themselves when there is such a blatant connection to a party involved in a case they are presiding over. While defending myself in a case where I was accused of assault for apprehending someone who stole some of my business equipment, the local judge asked me if I wanted him recused because the complainant grew up on the same street where he lived. Knowing that the facts were on my side, I told the judge that I trusted him to be impartial. The judge later ruled in my favor, citing a statute that allows the use of "reasonable force" when trying to recover stolen property.

Many judges will see your attempts to get them off the case as an insult. They will often fight to maintain a case they are steering in a particular direction due to their bias. They will find vague points of law that could be read to favor their position. They will use the excuse that if they had to recuse themselves for such loose relationships as you allege with pertinent parties, they would not be allowed to take the majority of cases they rule on.

The fact that Judge Barker served on the Board of Directors for Clarian Health Care Partners was crucial to my own argument for recusal, but it was not the only evidence of bias. I pointed to the official record of the case where Judge Barker approved an unconstitutional prior restraint, allowed the doctor to be his own expert witness, and ruled every step of the way in the doctor's favor, even going so far as denying a request to waive legal feels even when Lucille presented documentation that she lived only on disability checks. The judge, who received communications from Lucille's despicable sister Arlene (www.Arlenemulleysucks.com), found out that Lucille hired a lawyer because her sister made threats to sue her after the case against the doctor was well underway. She used this as evidence that Lucille could pay the court's filing fees and all the appeal filing fees.

I'd like to believe Judge Barker is an extreme case of what's wrong with our justice system, but I'm afraid the reality is that she is not such a rare bird. I also had another biased judge confess in open court to not reading the bulk of the material I submitted in the case after he took the litigation over for another judge who was just starting to warm up to me. His name was fitting: Judge King. It seemed to me like Judge King truly despised the fact that I represented myself and managed to do a halfway decent job. Judge King also repeatedly lamented that the case was taking up a lot of time and energy, and he made several attempts to get myself and the defendants to find some agreeable settlement. He obviously wanted it all to be over, so he did whatever he could to end it by denying my final request for relief without a fair hearing in which I was able to be heard. I had to appear by telephone, and the bulk of my remarks were garbled or omitted from the record because the connection with the court was horrible.

The one decent thing I can say about Judge King is that he did try to get me to work with the opposing lawyer. He also formally treated me at times like a peer of that attorney, which was somewhat flattering. Of course, Judge King would never ask me to draft an order for him to sign, but he did ask me to work with the other lawyer to make sure one particularly important order was not over-reaching. Though I voiced my objections to the draft to the opposition, they did nothing to change it, and the judge signed it anyway. I can't even count the amount of times I violated that specific order, but none of those violations were ever brought to the court's attention.

The counsel for the defendants I went after even told a sob story to the judge at one of the final hearings, claiming my work caused his casino-operating clients a ton of headaches with the state gaming commission. I immediately objected, stating that nothing I ever wrote about the Fertitta family was ever formally challenged in court or otherwise by his clients.

To this day, I have never been asked to remove any post or any part of a post I created by any member of the Fertitta family or any of their legal representatives. One of my posts about the Fertittas ended up being completely removed from a site called "Bleacher Report" once it reached around 13,500 reads, but the explanation the administrators gave me mentioned nothing about factual errors of any kind. They simply argued that they could not support any type of investigative reporting on the site. Someone who referred to himself as the site's "Content Moderation Coordinator" sent me a formal email containing the following paragraph:

"We do not allow writers to break their own news or investigative research on sensitive matters. Since you last spoke out on this issue three years ago on the site, we have strengthened our sourcing standards, so while your research may be correct, we unfortunately cannot accept it here anymore due to the discussed standards."

So, basically they admitted to me they were only going to publish fluff pieces backed by links to other established mainstream sites, and they obviously wanted no part of anyone on their site reporting the hard truth behind one of the most powerful sports leagues in the world. I remain convinced that someone connected to the Fertittas through the UFC or Station Casinos contacted the folks at Bleacher Report and threatened to cut off access to their events or pull their advertising from the site if my piece did not disappear.

The same administrator from the site responded to me once again when I asked for clarity on which parts of the removed piece would need to be changed. He told me the problem was not any particular statement or section of the piece. The issue was with the whole article. "We don't have the infrastructure to responsibly stand behind any investigative journalism. This isn't permitted from any writer under our current policies," he added.

Thankfully, there is something called The Internet Archive. I first started using the site when it called itself "The Wayback Machine." Upon discovering that Bleacher Report removed the piece, I found a copy in the archive:

http://web.archive.org/web/20121018190622/http:/bleacherreport.com/articles/119377-the-real-story-behind-the-ufcs-royal-family

So, even if you have a biased judge like I did who decides you have to remove all posts about your adversary, there is a way you can still share these posts with the masses. Even as an established writer with a long record of impeccable reporting at two newspapers and all across the Internet for various sites, I could not seem to generate any serious interest in my predicament from mainstream media outlets. An obscure New York magazine called "The Deal" featured a piece about the Xyience case, but my quotes were reduced once again to a fraction of the entire interview I completed with the writer. A huge site like Bleacher Report cowered in the face of adversity, and they sold their soul to mediocrity by deciding to eliminate all independent reporting and investigative journalism efforts.

The feeling I experienced after the last public advocacy group lawyer I reached out to refused to take the Xyience case over for me was virtually identical to how I felt after all my interviews on the subject were made into print pieces. The only exceptions were the posts on fightopinion.com, which were put together by one of the smartest writers in sports today. Zach Arnold took the time to research all the facts and had plenty of experience with investigative reporting of his own. He is so far the only person who did any justice to my story outside of folks who posted my unedited audio interviews.

I reached out to a lawyer from Public Citizen to see if he would take the Xyience case not long after it landed in my lap. He humored me for a while and maintained a line of communication, but he also told me he would have to see all the case material and all the articles I was being sued over. I spent a few days compiling a phone book of material to send over to him, and I rode a bicycle in a vicious downpour to get it all to the post office. I think it was less than a week later when I received a message from the attorney stating he was not interested.

The best way to describe that sense of rejection and how I dealt with it is to use the exact words I said at the time, which I borrowed from the movie Major League:

https://www.youtube.com/watch?v=UsjoFZEwAyI

Like Pedro Cerrano, I did it myself from that point on, and I worked harder than I ever did in my life to keep the case itself going while maintaining my reporting efforts at the same time. Because of the odds I faced, I don't blame that lawyer for not helping me, and I still kept in touch with him from time to time. He actually did provide me with some key observations, lessons about appeals, and sincere advice. I consulted him about Lucille's case as well. Looking back on the gentleman's communications I discovered this gem from his rejection email:

"Although it is galling to think about dropping allegations that you are certain are true, you would be very unwise to head into the defense of a libel case some 2,000 miles from home if the evidentiary record is going to be as sparse as you suggest it may be, even for the best of reasons."

At this point in the case, the opposing attorney actually wanted to settle the case with me removing the contested articles voluntarily for a small sum. First it was "a box of sodas" offered as a joke, and then it went up to a thousand dollars. I went out on a limb and requested a million bucks. "I'll see you in court," said the poor sap who filed the initial suit. A few months later he was complaining that he was out $84,000 in legal fees for his unpaid work on the case. I also later intercepted communications he sent to the founder of Xyience admitting the injunction he sought against me would be easy for any decent lawyer to appeal and get overturned. Sadly, I didn't get those critical and damning communications until after the whole bankruptcy fiasco was over.

I could still sue the attorney himself for malicious prosecution, but it wouldn't be worth the time it would take to secure a judgment. Also, I'm sure he could make the case that being sued by Xyience turned out better than I ever thought it would despite not getting a huge judgment in the end. The whole experience actually made me a much better writer, and the anger and frustration the lawsuit brought out in me motivated me to dig deeper than ever into the real history of the Fertitta family. Instead of utilizing anonymous sources or those who were only willing to talk if I kept their name out of it, I began to seek out incriminating court documents. I looked up all the major parties involved in Xyience and found detailed litigation history for all the key players. All of them were previously involved in deals that were allegedly corrupt, shady or crooked. One group of players in the bankruptcy actually faced a claim of Civil RICO for one of their prior scams.

Over time, the fact that I was not absolutely crushed by all the Xyience lawyers seemed to help me gain a ton of credibility across combat sports media circles. The company's two CEOs actually flew me to New York City for UFC 78 "Validation." Back then, every event had a catch phrase or name to go with it. It's hilarious to me that the executives picked that named event to sit down with me and find out if I was serious. It was my writing more than anything that brought that meeting on. The company's founder was trying to make it difficult for the Fertittas to take the whole thing over, so they wanted me to write more about him being a total scumbag to help them bring the company through a planned bankruptcy. I managed to make a fast friend in the area who was with an investment firm, and I brought him to the meeting with me. He pretended like he wanted to invest in Xyience, and he made my job so much easier. I barely had to say a word.

My friend asked all the right questions, and even though I didn't take notes there were certain comments made by the executives I could never forget. At one point the investment guru asked them if they considered going door to door to investors to ask for capital. The company CEO laughed off the suggestion, admitting that the Fertittas were not interested in that approach. He followed that up by saying they would probably have to go "scorched earth." In other words, every shareholder would have to be wiped out.

They did still ask my friend how much money his firm could get if they needed it, and how soon. He told them a story about the Enron days when his firm provided one California power company a million dollars in 24 hours. One of their defenses to accusations of fraud they cited later pointed to all the different firms they sought out for capital investments. They of course listed my friend's company as one of the entities they sought funds from despite the fact that I delivered this guy to their lunch table and they never contacted him again. One question is not a serious effort to get investment capital.

Before the meeting ended, both executives told me they would see me at the fights, which were in New Jersey that night. I told them there was a problem. I didn't have enough cash to get to the fights. "What happened to the $500 we sent you," one of them asked. I pointed to the suit I was wearing. They both cracked a smiled first, and then each of them pulled a hundred dollar bill out of his pocket and put it on the table.

I later found out there was actually a private investigator watching the whole meeting from a distance. The PI happened to be bankrolled by a friend of the company founder. I would eventually come to the understanding that the founder and his close associates were actually the lesser of two evils. The Fertittas were much worse. Unlike the convicted felon who started Xyience, these shady brothers had the power and influence to avoid any criminal or civil liability for their most egregious schemes and scams. Xyience was just another conquest to them, and they didn't seem to care that over 380 shareholders saw their investments go up in smoke because they wanted the company all for themselves.

The evening of the fights I found one of the executives at the venue and was waiting to speak to him with a pile of documentation I was prepared to give him. Something gave me second thoughts, and I ended up keeping everything. Upon returning home I found a series of emails from a company insider who claimed to have an office right next to the Xyience's Chief Financial Officer. The witness overheard conversations in which executives discussed the need to prop Xyience up as a legitimate UFC sponsor as far into the bankruptcy as they could. The covenants of a multi-million-dollar loan and credit package hinged on the state of the business and the sponsors of the business. The emails I received convinced me to start looking into the executives who flew me to New York and wanted me to help with their "scorched earth" campaign. A whole group of key investors and new company executives actually ended up being tied to a major scandal involving cash-advance kiosks at casinos all over the world.

The two CEOS (the same Adam Frank and Kirk Sanford in the recording featured earlier in this book) eventually decided they could only offer me $5,000 to settle the case I filed against them as a counterclaim and drop the initial suit against me. There was no sense in me taking that offer no matter how bad I needed the money at the time. Instead, I filed a detailed sanctions motion outlining how the whole case against me resulted due to a desperate need to hide the fraud key players were committing behind the scenes at Xyience. The more I learned about all the different people who came into Xyience to try to straighten things out, the more I realized this company was an easy target. There was one scam on top of another perpetrated by some of those trusted to fix things.

I later found out Mark Cuban, the owner of the Dallas Mavericks and co-star of "*Shark Tank*," actually read some of my case documents when he was trying to get Randy Couture to sign with his own fledgling fight league. He ended up being a major investor in that financing package the Fertittas secured for themselves. That package allowed the UFC to purchase PRIDE, their main competitor at the time. Much of the remaining money went into the pockets of the Fertitta Brothers and UFC President Dana White.

I reached out to Cuban first when I heard about the situation with Couture, who was in a serious feud with his former UFC bosses at the time. Cuban responded within a few days with the following (the typos are his own):

I've been following your battle w them

I have to say, I don't see how them paying them,selves by investing in xyience, even if its an inflated sponsorship, is wrong, since both companies are private

Now if they mislead bankers w incorrect figures, that's different. Lyong to a bank is a huge problem. But if I invest in your site and you then buy ads from me, that happens every day

It wasn't only the gaming commission and Mark Cuban that ended up being interested in my work. The Bankruptcy Trustee assigned to the Xyience case quickly figured out I had key information he needed to build his case. He provided funds for me to travel to Illinois to meet the man who would be the counsel for the case near that attorney's home office. I spent the better part of two days speaking with Attorney Jonathan Backman, and I finally started believing there might be some decent and honest lawyers in this world. The case was so wide-ranging and complicated that he had to file multiple civil complaints to try to recover everything he could for the creditors.

There was never any hope for getting anything back for the shareholders, as bankruptcy rules place creditors at the head of the pack for recovery. The shareholders typically only get something in a bankruptcy if there's enough cash for the creditors to be paid in full. Still, I felt compelled to do my own part to get them the funds they deserved since the evidence showed it was the Fertittas who promised to invest at least $15 million into Xyience if my stories were removed from the Internet. I contended that it was my silence during the initial litigation period (the injunction left me convinced for a few weeks that I was better off holding off on my writing until I figured out all the legal nuances) that allowed the Fertittas to pull off what the trustee's counsel called their "loan to own scheme."

The lawsuit against me specifically stated there were major investors willing to provide funds but only if my "defamatory postings" were removed from cyberspace. Essentially, the suit was only brought forward for the purposes of getting the initial preliminary injunction to take effect long enough to satisfy the Fertittas and get their money into the business to prevent a bankruptcy.

Fertitta Enterprises was the entity that made the investment in Xyience and then took it over as soon as the first loan payment didn't get paid. There is no Web-site for this company and little to find online about it outside my own work. It is essentially a holding company for Fertitta family investments and other major assets. They even created a whole new entity called Zyen, LLC in order to reconstitute the Xyience brand after a group of "stalking horse bidders" defaulted on what was obviously a hollow agreement to begin with. Fertitta Enterprises actually has a substantial litigation history, and much of the lawsuits against them had some truly damaging evidence against the casino barons regarding their deceptive business practices. "Follow the money" is not just good advice for an investigative reporter, it's a universal commandment.

Now, as much as I would love to tell the whole stories behind the corruption at Xyience and Lucille's tragic experience with elective surgery right here, this is not the right place for all that. Let's take a moment to discuss the final piece of the publication puzzle.

How do you go about making your case interesting and generating a healthy following of people who can relate to it? I have two words to answer that question: be creative. If you have no writing skills you probably will not make it as a self-represented party in the first place. Most people who do think they are capable of learning the ropes by themselves without a law school curriculum find out the hard way that it really is an impossible task. If you don't have a certain knack for writing at the outset you might be better off just trying to find the cheapest lawyer out there. If you can write well, this chapter is tailor made for you.

If you are not great at creating Web-sites or blogs, go with a company that provides a very simple and user-friendly interface. The quickest way to get the attention of your adversaries is to populate your site or your blog with all the details you can assemble about your position in the case. Remember to stick to the facts. Also remember that you can use a variety of sites to host your documents for free. I stand by docstoc.com, and instead of labeling each document with the title it has on the court docket, I came up with my own creative titles like the one I gave to this order laying out the ridiculous sanctions Lucille faced for refusing to remove everything she wrote about the doctor from her blog:

http://www.docstoc.com/docs/25032217/Judge-Sarah-Evans-Barker-Strikes-Major-Federal-Blow-to-Free-Speech

If you know nothing about SEO, try visiting www.fiverr.com once your blog or full-fledged site is up and running. If you'd rather voice your concerns on other sites related to the type of case you are involved in, keep the URL of the post close at hand and try to get it in front of as many eyeballs as you possibly can. Fiverr offers very affordable and potent SEO services and massively important social site marketing offerings. If you want to use a site like Facebook, make a fan page and find someone on Fiverr to get it a few thousand "likes." Go to a popular forum on the same subject that surrounds your litigation stream and leave a post linking to the main documents involved.

If you do create your own site, it might take more than Fiverr's help to get it to the top of Google's search engines. You might need a complete makeover by a trained SEO specialist to maximize your site's potential. I get emails from at least two or three of these specialized companies each day, all promising to get me on the first page of Google. It took thousands of dollars and years of work for the folks behind Xyience to get my own sites related to Xyience to stop appearing on the first page of Google searches for "Xyience." For the bulk of the early part of the case, my main page was ranked third in Google searches. These days it is in the cellar of the third page of searches. Since I forward the Xyiencesucks.com site right now to a Blogger platform, the hits do not register like they would if all my content was physically hosted on xyiencesucks.com with a Wordpress blog.

Since the company is under new ownership now, it's really not the time to try to get www.xyiencesucks.com back up to the number three spot:

http://www.cagepotato.com/xyience-sold-to-big-red-will-no-longer-be-an-official-ufc-sponsor/

So, I'm OK with the blog being more obscure now that the lawsuit is over. If I ever ramp it up again it will be to promote the book I'll be writing on the subject to help benefit all those burned shareholders. Then it will be like starting the whole publication effort over again. I will go back to where I started, with a simple press release.

There are also a growing number of press release sites that allow you to create free press releases. For a more substantial fee you can get your PR sent to hundreds of different media outlets all across the country. For free you might just get your statement posted to an obscure link somewhere. You will have to generate the traffic for yourself.

The major social sites are a must when it comes to populating your links and getting eyeballs on your content. This is where a little creativity comes in handy. Try to learn how to edit photos and create intriguing videos for a more visual appeal. Read anything you can about how a post goes "viral." Study the best videos and blogs on similar subjects.

Chances are you will not have to expose billionaires or a major company with a strong web presence like I had to. During Lucille's case it was much easier to get sites I created to appear at the top of search results for pertinent terms. Though many of them were eliminated precisely because they appeared so high on the search engines, I knew that creating them would piss off the lawyers and judges involved along with my actual adversaries trying to improperly gain protection from my "future speech" by abusing the courts. I knew Judge Barker would rule in anger rather than after careful reflection of the law when I published judgegod.com about her unconstitutional orders. I really felt the only way to expose her bias and complete misrepresentation of the law was to get her to continue to overstep her bounds. I knew she would make a mistake or two in the long run trying to keep me quiet, and an appeal would settle everything.

Tragically, Lucille died before the case ended while she faced insurmountable obstacles at every turn. She had one last chess move that left everything in my hands, though somehow her evil sister managed to take over defense of the case on behalf of Lucille's estate. It didn't take me long to get searches for "Arlene Mulley" on Google to return my site as the top search result. For years Mulley used to randomly call me and hang up, flush a toilet in the background, or scream something quickly and hang up. She sometimes even left grating messages with a disturbing voice that annoyed me to no end. The most sensible word to describe Arlene that I can think of is "diabolical," but I also would contend that she borders on demonic. I wouldn't be surprised if it turned out that this woman is actually the Anti-Christ in the flesh.

I use a company called HootSuite to manage all my social network postings, and rather than just automate my own blogs to post links on all my networks I also populate the links of other related blogs that compete with my sites. This way my network sites become resources for fans of the fighting sports. You can even set up a Wordpress blog to automatically post content from other sites within your blog like they are part of your site.

The basic concept of SEO is mostly related to the ratio of incoming and outgoing links. A site gains popularity for a search term in a search engine due to a variety of factors. Sometimes it is as simple as the domain name. If you are a boxing manager and register the domain boxingmanager.com, you don't have to have outstanding amounts of ingoing and outgoing links to your site in order to appear high in searches for "boxing manager" on Google. People will simply stumble across the site even if they are not looking for it specifically. If you can't register a name that will return the best results possible, you will need to have some kind of blog platform with a bunch of posts that will draw folks in. The posts will then become "incoming" links. Many sites will have a dotcom landing page with a button you press to bring you to the blog. I like to make my actual site the blog with Wordpress. Place a list of links in the sidebar somewhere with the label "Friends of Our" Site or something along those lines. Link to a long list of related sites and contact each one to see if they will link back to you.

Back when I first started fighting the Xyience case, MySpace was still fairly popular. I used an auto-adder program to add tons of friends to a group of profiles I created. I used the same program to leave thousands of comments on other pages leading people to content about the lawsuit. If you can populate your social networks with a little affordable help from Fiverr, you can use a program like HootSuite to blast your links out across the World Wide Web.

You don't have to be great at investigative reporting, but you do need to keep your facts straight and be somewhat entertaining to hold any audience's sustained interest. Most people prefer to read writing that is more conversational in tone and flow.

You don't even have to write a full article. I found success on Docstoc by writing "Open Letters" to both Judge Barker (she had it removed) and Mr. Backman (http://www.docstoc.com/docs/51933137/Open-Letter-to-Xyience-BK-Estate-Counsel-Jon-Backman). You cannot get anywhere in court by sending an actual written letter to the judge. It's not something she can legally weigh in the process as actual evidence. Making it an open letter makes it a public statement more than a personal one. At the same time, the only reason I wrote an open letter to Judge Barker was because I knew there was no hope of her seeing the light or coming to an epiphany. She always did side with the doctor from her home state and always would. There was nothing I could do but make her mad enough to go after me, hoping my doing so would take some heat off Lucille. She eventually ruled that the case itself, which was generating bad publicity for Eppley in the local media as well as Online, could not be written about at all and no filings could be posted anywhere online.

Typically such a gag order is only needed for extreme circumstances where lives may be in danger or some other serious risk is taken by way of publicizing a court case. This case was absolutely unconstitutional, as there was absolutely no cause to restrict the record from public consumption. Forbidding me from writing anything about the case amounted to a clear "prior restraint" that Judge Barker could not have sustained if I were able to appeal her rulings directly on my own behalf instead of for Lucille only. As a trained and established writer, the courts would have to treat me differently than even a well-educated and intelligent older woman like Lucille. This is not to say her speech would have been generally subject to more restrictions on free speech than mine, but at the same time I had a track record of solid reporting with no accusations of any prior misconduct at either of the two major newspapers I worked at in Massachusetts and New Hampshire.

I had very little written content about Lucille Online before the case began. None of my online posts were actually subject to injunction when the doctor's attorneys obtained the first preliminary injunction. There was nothing published in print yet, either. With Lucille there was a ton of content already in print they sought to restrict. When it came to me, they only wanted to prevent me from publishing what I "might" write someday in the future.

Once I met with the trustee's counsel in the Xyience case, the case Xyience filed against me was all but over. I knew he would never pursue the claims, so the courts could not use those accusations against me, especially not when I secured a $5,000 judgment from the trustee as a result of my sanctions motion that charged the entire case was frivolous from the outset. All prior injunctions became moot, but getting deals done in bankruptcy is not very easy. Attorney Backman and I butted heads on occasion, and that's why I ultimately felt the need to call him out in public with the open letter. His behavior changed for the better after that.

Judge Barker's open letter would not change her mind or her treatment of Lucille. I knew that when I wrote it. What it did do was get her to write another unconstitutional order demanding the letter be removed from cyberspace.

The more content I saw removed from the Internet, the more I realized what I was doing had a major effect on the judge and my opposition in the Eppley case. Even though I didn't voluntarily delete anything beyond a few posts on my Fight News Unlimited blog (after they shut down the whole site to get rid of a few posts), Judge Barker later rescinded many of the contempt fees she levied against me after her own restrictive court orders shut those posts and sites down. Still, a close look at some of the docket entries provides a bit of a glimpse at what kind of legal threats I faced for my resistance of the judge's rulings:

http://www.plainsite.org/dockets/kfcsbf4f/indiana-southern-district-court/eppley-md-dmd-v-iacovelli/

It is also a great idea to concentrate on trying to reach your adversary's peers. If a judge, attorney or opposing party is trying to wipe his or her rear end with the Constitution after a particularly disgusting waste dump, share the story of what happened with colleagues of that person. It's easier to find lawyers and plastic surgeons to send emails to, but getting the attention of fellow judges might take some extra steps. There are sites like www.judicialwatch.org/ that cater to widespread corruption on a national scale. Smaller incidents may not get their attention, but you can learn a great deal about exposing corruption by studying how they operate.

Lucille's case had me so mad at how the doctor's attorneys were disrespecting the purpose of the justice system that I sent email blasts to hundreds of Indianapolis law firms (every lawyer at every firm I could find addresses for online). I sent them anonymously, but the doctor's lawyers quickly learned about what I was doing and tried to stop it.

I also sent long emails from my unmasked email address to the doctor himself and all his attorneys. As the case proceeded through the system, I had no idea it was likely all paid for by insurance a doctor has to maintain to be in practice in the first place. I figured the legal fees would cripple the doctor in the long run, as even reading an email from me would typically be something they could bill their client for.

The doctor paid his insurance premiums to the same Clarian Health Care entity where Judge Barker held a seat on the Board of Directors. As stacked as the system was against me, I refused to even imagine not succeeding on appeal and kept on writing as much as I could about the case. Lucille's death also meant an appeal would be impossible, though it also technically made the permanent injunction in the case unenforceable. The language of the restrictions forbids those "acting in concert" with Lucille from posting anything related to the case or the procedure that was the subject of the case. Unless I am an admitted and/or proven medium, there is no way for me to act in concert with a person who is dead.

Ultimately, there will be whole books written about all the nuances of both cases. The litigation is over, but justice was never properly served in either case. The process of providing that justice by exposing all parties that prevented it for so long is perfect in this scenario. Lucille may not be here to witness it, but her story will live on. Xyience shareholders may be suffering now, but someday my creative efforts surrounding my work on the case will hopefully provide just enough revenue to guarantee each investor some meaningful recovery by way of proceeds from my book sales and the potential for a movie or documentary to launch about it all after the book goes out.

Before you jump into the legal process head first, you need to know that it sometimes takes an incredible amount of time and effort to get to the end of the road you're about to go down. It will sometimes feel like you're Andy Dufresne from the movie *Shawshank Redemption*, digging your way out of prison with a tiny rock hammer, chipping away a little more each night after dark. After all that, you might have to crawl through your own version of an active sewer pipe to finally accomplish your goal. Being your own lawyer is ugly, messy, and certainly not for everyone.

Harnessing the incredible power of publication may be the only way you can even the odds against an attorney with a wealthy client. You will have to find the least expensive way to fight back, and often that's the kind of work you just cannot accomplish through the courts, especially if you are dealing with people who are not above corrupting judges. Registering a domain name or starting a blog to advocate for yourself and expose your opposition is not going to drain your bank account. Emailing and calling news outlets to try to get your story picked up is just going to cost you your time.

The legal system, like many of the most corrupt systems in the world, is all about the money. The person who can spend the least to get the best results can usually win as long as corruption and plain bad luck doesn't get in the way. To get results when you just don't have the level of training your opposition does, you have to find an advantage you have that they aren't so familiar with.

Most lawyers are far from having the creative writing talent of famed Novelist John Grisham. The typical attorney is probably not going to even oppose or counter your creative efforts outside of court. The client might try that if they are smart enough to know they need to, but a lawyer's job is to use the courts to get what his client wants.

At the same time, a lawyer's reputation is important to him, so if he or she is abusing the law to help a client, let the public know. Name and shame the lawyers on the case, too. If you can't get to the client, maybe you will at least convince the lawyer it is not worth destroying his chances of keeping future clients after they do some research on him and find your content that exposes him as the scum of the earth.

If you legitimately have the time and energy to put into fighting your legal battles on two fronts, the one-front your opposition is fighting will be no match for you. If your case is important enough for you and could also help others in similar predicaments if you can win, there's no excuse not to do everything you can to get that victory. Also, you absolutely should never forget that your story may be worth more than the case itself in the long run. This is especially true if you just need to defend yourself and do not have a counterclaim against your opposition. Sometimes even if you win in court, it may not be satisfying enough without people knowing the full story. All in all, putting your story out there in addition to your court documents is a win-win situation. From my experience, I can honestly say that the court of public opinion can do more for you than any legal court on the planet.

I can also tell you that I would not be in any position to give any advice about the legal system if it wasn't for my creative efforts being the equalizer in the Xyience case. Back when I had no idea what I was doing as my own attorney, I had to rely on my strengths as a blogger. The more attention the story received, the more people were willing to help me out with the legal nuances. Even if you do not have the writing experience I came into the legal system with, a big enough story will sell itself, even if written badly. Unless you have a real passion for the law, learning to effectively get your message across though creative efforts will probably be much easier than being your own attorney.

The pen truly is mightier than the sword, but whoever originally said that would be in stupendous awe of how powerful the written word is today thanks to the World Wide Web. We live in a world where one tweet could potentially transform a complete nobody into a superstar overnight. Think about all the stories that end up making it into the 24-hour news cycle where a victim of some unfortunate circumstance is profiled. Often, these folks start up a funding campaign that goes viral as a result of the exposure, and that gets them out of whatever trouble they're in.

It's all about persistence and work ethic in the long run. Everything worth accomplishing in life is difficult. You just have to keep chipping away one bit at a time, and eventually all your hard work will pay off with a judgment in your favor or the loud bang of a judge's gavel followed by two very important words: "case dismissed!"

CONCLUSION:

Trial and Error

If your case makes it to a trial, that can be the most daunting part of any legal effort. Instead of going to a hearing once a month for a half-hour or so each time, all of a sudden you might have to spend a full day or more in court trying to get all your facts and evidence into a nice tight package any judge or jury could relate to. You will have to study up on questioning witnesses, introducing exhibits, and when and how to object.

The trial is likely going to be where your opponent will have to spend the most money if he or she hired an expensive attorney. Most clients will want to avoid those outrageous hourly fees if they can. Right before a case is scheduled for a trial is probably the best time to negotiate a settlement. Unfortunately, most settlements will contain a non-disclosure clause. You might never be able to tell anyone how much money you were able to walk away with, and the other side will typically not have to admit any wrongdoing.

If your case is one that cries out for taking full advantage of the publication route, try to avoid agreeing to anything that makes it impossible to market all that work you did to get your hard-fought victory. Better yet, avoid a trial by putting enough evidence, written testimony and facts on the record for you to be able to file a "summary judgment" motion. This is a detailed package that explains why there is no need to go through a trial because the facts that are crucial to the case are undisputed.

Ultimately, being your own attorney can be very rewarding. You may have to work twice as hard as the legal representative facing you, but a win will also feel twice as good to you. The attorney still gets paid no matter what in most cases. At best, all they can hope for is a hefty percentage of the judgment and the judge forcing you to pay for their attorney fees instead of their client.

I am a firm believer in the concept that whatever does not kill you only makes you stronger. There's also a great chance that the reason you had to represent yourself in the first place is due to a lack of financial resources. In that scenario, even if the opposition wins, collecting what you owe will be like trying to get blood from a stone. Above all, you never know when you might have to call on your legal skills again. That trying experience of defending yourself or launching your own case against someone might really help you if you ever get in another legal bind. Experiencing failure is often what spurs the world's greatest innovators and success stories.

My own situation is a prime example. The Xyience case came along around three years before Lucille's debacle landed in my lap. It seemed to me as if all this was happening for some divine reason. This was my fate, and what might have made other writers distraught and upset was my badge of courage. I embraced the concept of being sued and realized that it was not happening because I was a lying hack. People were suing me because I was hitting them where it hurt and making it harder for them to get away with their worst behavior without accepting the consequences of their actions.

My legal struggles cost me a few thousand dollars of my own money to come out without any major losses. It might not seem worth the effort or expense to outside observers looking at my situation, but it's a lot better than trying to figure out how to pay off a $25 million judgment. I still had a story I could tell when the smoke cleared, too. Actually, I have a few stories.

Most importantly, my predicament taught me enough so that I can help other people in the same dire situation that resulted in me writing this book. This effort and my gripe sites will no doubt help and inspire others to beat the odds. I will never forget how hopeless and helpless reading that initial complaint made me feel. Going from zero legal knowledge to actually possessing some limited legal prowess took some serious resolve and plenty of grunt work. All of it was worth it.

Judges will discourage you, opposing lawyers will underestimate you, and the system will intimidate you at the beginning. It's easy to think that making any progress is impossible. On the contrary, just surviving long enough to put together a decent case is going to impress a judge or jury if it comes from you. Little is expected of you, so make sure you exceed those expectations. It will also really sting the opposing lawyer if you can start stringing together a few rulings in your favor. Here he is after spending his trust fund on the best law school he could get into only to watch you come in with no formal training at all and walk all over him.

Judges tend to look down on self-represented parties because they lack patience and hate to have to explain the system to outsiders. They want to deal with someone who paid their dues and speaks their language. They will sometimes look at you like you're an ant challenging an elephant to a fight. Exhibit some patience of your own and stumble your way through the beginning stages with the idea that it can only get better if you keep working at it and stay focused on the ultimate goal.

I really hope this book can help you realize that your own personal legal nightmare is not so scary after all. I also hope you understand going in that it may be called "The Justice System," but justice is often not the byproduct it produces. Sometimes it only gives the person needing it to work for him nothing but headaches and aggravation.

There will be a time when you question why you bothered to handle your case on your own in the first place. You will be overworked and stressed out just trying to keep your head above water as you try to learn the ropes. You will ask yourself a hundred times if it's really worth it or if you should just give up. Don't quit. You will never forgive yourself if there's even the slightest chance that something good could come out of you giving it an honest shot.

At the same time, the worst thing you can fall victim to in the legal process is thinking you can do it ALL alone. Get help wherever you can, and get it at the cheapest rate you can. If you're a good person at heart and you have a good cause, people will not need much convincing to assist you. Some people might even help you without charging you a dime, just like I did for Lucille.

Looking back at my own legal adventures, I certainly have regrets and moments I wish I could go back and relive. I made mistakes, and I paid for them. What separated me from other pro-se parties was the fact that I knew how to find the facts and precedent cases that exonerated me and get them on the record.

My greatest inspiration to keep up the fight was not monetary gain. Greed was precisely what made my opposition such scumbags and scam artists. I didn't need money to make me feel like I won against those folks. I just needed the satisfaction of knowing I could prevent people from silencing my best work. In many ways, winning a bunch of money would have been the worst thing for me. That would have made it easier to forget how much work there is still left to do.

I am not a lawyer. I'm a writer. What was always most valuable to me was the same thing that motivated Lucille to wake up every morning and write. She wanted to help other people. So do I. There is nothing that feels as awesome as doing everything in your power to support an altruistic cause.

Unfortunately, there was not much I could do to turn back the tide of corruption and pure evil that ultimately drowned Lucille. Her case was a stark example of systematic torture perpetrated by the wealthy and powerful on a poor, defenseless individual through the improper use of the courts as an agent and instrument of intimidation. She showed me that free speech can truly be a matter of life and death. Her tragic suicide proved to me that our justice system can be incredibly toxic, and the fact that there are far too many people who get away with the abuse of that system motivated me more than anything to write this book.

Lawyers will not fix this system. It is a game for too many of them, and they get paid to play it well. For people like Lucille and myself, there was absolutely no chance to receive fair treatment or earn a favorable judgment from such a biased and corrupt judge. Lawyers play the game, and the judges sometimes make up the rules as they go. Since only appeals can remedy such a situation and the appeals process is so convoluted and complicated, most judges know they can get away with shafting a self-represented party in favor of helping out a member of the club who paid his dues and passed the bar.

The only way this kind of horrendous system can change for the better is for more people to refuse to accept the status quo. Stand up for your rights and take charge of your own case. Do not let some schmuck in a cheap suit or fancy robe force you to give up your rights to due process and your hard-earned money. That only perpetuates the problems that plague the legal profession. It is time to realize that you deserve much better than what this busted system traditionally provides, and only you can make sure you get it.